The Bootleg Homes
OF
Frank Lloyd Wright

The Bootleg Homes
OF
Frank Lloyd Wright

HIS CLANDESTINE WORK REVEALED

ROBERT J. HARTNETT

THE
History
PRESS

Published by The History Press
Charleston, SC
www.historypress.com

Front cover, center left: Blueprint courtesy of the Frank Lloyd Wright Foundation Archives (The Museum of Modern Art | Avery Architectural & Fine Arts Library, Columbia University, New York).

First published 2023

Manufactured in the United States

ISBN 9781467154062

Library of Congress Control Number: 2022951596

boot·leg·ger (noun): a person who makes, distributes, or sells goods illegally
—Oxford Languages

Contents

Introduction

When someone hears the phrase "Chicago bootlegger," they might conjure up images of Al Capone, the man who controlled most of Chicago's illegal liquor trade during the Roaring Twenties.

People might not readily think of Frank Lloyd Wright as a bootlegger; they will likely remember the grand Prairie-style houses he designed, or the summer home for Edgar Kaufmann called Falling Water or even Taliesin or Taliesin West.

The homes that Wright nicknamed his bootleg commissions were completed in the early 1890s, almost twenty-seven years before the real Chicago bootleggers were making headlines for their exploits. Capone, his friends, and his rivals were glorified in newspaper headlines; Capone thought of himself as a modern-day Robin Hood, even though J. Edgar Hoover had placed him at the top of the FBI's "Most Wanted" list. Maybe Frank Lloyd Wright liked to suggest he, too, was a well-dressed socialite, able to come and go as he pleased, hobnobbing with the rich and famous of the day and being the center of attention regardless of the circumstances, just like those speakeasy gangsters.

I have tried to present the information contained herein with as much accuracy as possible. We must keep in mind that there has been some confusion as to the dates of Wright's early commissions and some of the events that occurred in his life.

To address the misunderstandings regarding the dates given to Wright's commissions, the reader must be aware of four points that are linked to Wright's early career.

(1) Some projects were dated to the time when drawings were first commissioned, while others have been dated to the time the buildings were constructed.

(2) Building permits for Wright's early commission were never issued or have been lost or destroyed.

(3) Some commissions have been given an identification number from the Frank Lloyd Wright Foundation Archives, even though the project is also included in the catalog of works of Adler & Sullivan; and finally,

(4) Neither Frank Lloyd Wright nor the people who were the first ones to place his works in chronological order were exempt from human error.

John O. Holzhueter addressed the issue of how the determinations for the original dates of Wright's work were chronicled in his 1988 article in the *Wisconsin Magazine of History*.

I think Holzhueter's comments on this issue are well articulated, and I include an excerpt from his article here:

> *Wright was a busy man, preoccupied with work and the necessity of meeting professional and financial obligations.*

This sentence is straightforward; it does not contain any ambiguities. The same cannot be said for the following sentence, which reads as follows (emphasis mine):

> *His chronologies and* dates went askew, *not because of some overall plot* (though there may be exceptions), *but simply because* he and others forgot details *or* reshaped them *along the lines of long-held impressions and* faulty recollections.

The second sentence gives not just one phrase that raises suspicion, but five. "Dates went askew": this phrase suggests that dates were mistakenly recorded out of order. The phrase "though there may be exceptions" implies that misdating may have been done on purpose. The last three emphasized comments—Wright and others "forgot details" or "reshaped them," and there were "faulty recollections"—all point to someone(s) involvement in publishing dates that were inaccurate.

Other authors have tried to label which commissions were thought to have been bootleg designs, but these authors have not included all the commissions from this phase of Wright's career, or they have included commissions that, at the time, may have been suspected to have been bootleg commissions but since have had the dates of the project revised to place them either prior to the time Wright's bootleg phase began or after the phase was over.

The only database that lists all of Wright's work, including both built and unbuilt commissions, is the Frank Lloyd Wright Foundation Archives. One book that uses the data from Wright's archives to list his commissions is the book by Bruce Brooks Pfeiffer and Peter Goessel, *Frank Lloyd Wright. Complete Works. Vol. 1, 1885–1916.*

Based on the research completed, I will try to determine which of the fourteen commissions from 1890 through 1894 that have been proposed as bootlegs deserve to be labeled as such.

To present the material discussed in this book in a sensible order, I have listed the commissions and projects by location (Chicago, Illinois; La Grange, Illinois; Oak Park, Illinois) and then by the number assigned to the work by the Frank Lloyd Wright Foundation Archives, which are held at the Avery Architectural and Fine Arts Library, Columbia University, New York.

Wright may have created the numbering system himself, or it may have been the formula provided by the University of Wisconsin's Engineering Department for dating documents. As we will come to find out, Wright was enrolled at this university for two semesters, in 1885 and 1886.

Wright's first three recorded drawings are from his time as a college student. His first recorded drawing is numbered 8501.01. The number 85 stands for the year 1885. The number 01 references the project number for that year. The number .01 stands for the number of drawings done for a particular project.

Wright rarely included on his plan sheets which month during a particular year a commission was (1) received, (2) begun or (3) completed. For these dates, other sources must be researched, including trade journals, where projects were announced; newspaper articles that reported on real estate transactions and construction news; and correspondence between a client and the architect, if available.

Very often, there is no empirical evidence of the exact date of a commission. In these cases, family archives or personal histories may need to be consulted.

The numbering system used in the volume for the works of Adler & Sullivan is derived from the same classification numbers used in the book titled *The Complete Architecture of Adler & Sullivan*, written by Richard Nickel and Aaron Siskind with help from John Vinci and Ward Miller, published by the Richard Nickol Committee in 2010.

Today, the numbers for Wright's collection of drawings have had another decimal place added. Therefore, the correct number for Wright's first drawing is now considered to be 8501.001.

For the commissions being reviewed here, only the primary four-digit numbers will be listed, unless one of a collection of drawn documents includes pertinent information. The Frank Lloyd Wright archives uses the word *project* to identify unbuilt work; wherever possible, I have tried to use this definition also.

To put Wright's bootleg phase in the context of Wright's employment, our review should begin when he was first employed by Adler & Sullivan in 1887. However, as we will see, there are instances prior to 1887 when Wright names himself as a draftsman when he was only an office clerk and when he titles himself as an architect when he was just a draftsman.

In 1897, Illinois became the first state in the Union to establish a licensing act for architects; prior to that time, anyone designing buildings in Illinois could call themselves an architect. Wright was not saying anything that was not true per se; it is just that his employer may not have given him the same title.

Prelude

1825 TO 1866

William C. Wright and His Nomadic Life

*William C. Wright was not a genius like his son, but his journeyman
compositions are not without their earnest charms.*
*—Ken Emerson, commenting on the record album of works composed by
William C. Wright*

William C. Wright, the man who would become Frank Lloyd Wright's father, was born in Westfield, Massachusetts, in 1825, where his father was a Baptist minister. Westfield is located one hundred miles southwest of Boston, Massachusetts, near the city of Springfield. His future wife, Permelia, was also born in 1825, to Albern and Elizabeth Holcomb. She was raised on her parents' farm in Herkimer County, New York. William and Permelia met in Utica, New York, where William was teaching music after graduating college. It was from here that William and Permelia Wright began their nomadic and—yet unknown to them—tragic family life. In the mid-1800s, the infant mortality rate in the United States was near 22 percent, and this heartbreaking truth did not escape the Wright family. Their first child was born and subsequently died on May 23, 1854,

Left: William Wright. *Right*: Permelia Wright. *Courtesy of the William C. Wright Collection, State Historical Society of Iowa, Iowa City, and Hope Rogers.*

while the couple was living in Hartford, Connecticut. The family had moved to Hartford so William could study law. He was sustaining the family on the meager income he achieved from teaching piano lessons and passing the hat at the sermons he provided at various lecture halls. It was said that William had a commanding presence, and when he spoke on the ways of the Lord, people listened.

The Wrights' second and third children, both sons—Charles, born in 1854, and George, born in 1856—survived to adulthood. Charles was born while the family was still living in Hartford, which can be found on the west side of the Connecticut River. By the time George was born, the family had moved to East Hartford, located on the opposite side of the river. William must have been persuaded by the news from America's western frontier as he and other young families began to leave the comforts of eastern cities to become pioneers in what was to become a wave of western expansion.

In 1860, William moved his wife and their small family west, first to Iowa, where they came to stay in the town of Bell Plaine. On their travels west, Permelia was found to be "with child" again, and on the tenth of July, their daughter Elizabeth Amelia was born.

The family did not stay long in Iowa; soon, they were off to Lone Rock, Wisconsin, where the family was welcomed as William sought out work. It is not known why they came to Lone Rock or even why they left Iowa. But these western towns were growing, and William, having made somewhat of a name for himself as a preacher, could always find work among the spiritual pioneers. William did find work as a preacher and became a respected member of the Lone Rock community, but his salary was not keeping pace with the needs of his household. The family began to take on boarders. One such boarder was a young Welsh schoolteacher named Anna Lloyd Jones. Anna's family had settled in Richland Center, Wisconsin, which was only sixteen miles northwest of Lone Rock. As a teacher in rural Wisconsin, Anna would travel on horseback from one farmstead to another, supplying lesson plans for children of all ages. In the summer of 1863, Permelia was with child again, and the little bundle was expected to be born in February the following year. Wisconsin winters are cold and snowy, and the conditions in February 1864 were typically wintry.

The temperatures in February that year never broke the freezing mark and hovered around twenty-five degrees all month. During the first few days of February, Permelia went into labor. The baby's birthday was not recorded, and the infant struggled to make its way into the world until February 6, when the poor child took its last breath. Permelia's grief must have been overwhelming, because she joined her two babies in eternal rest just two months later.

William must have been beside himself; he had no extended family in Wisconsin to help him raise his three children. He needed a new wife, and the children needed a mother. Whether it was a matter of convenience or love, or even luck, William needed to look no further than his own home for his next wife: the young woman who was renting a room would certainly be suitable for both roles. William and Anna were married in 1866. After the marriage, William continued to move his family from one town to another in search of a position as a preacher. The family first moved to Richland Center, Wisconsin, where Anna could keep in close contact with her family. Her parents and brothers all had established farms in and around Richland Center. This small farming town was where William and Anna's first child was born.

1863 TO 1888

Frank Lloyd Wright's Formative Years

*Early in life, I had to choose between honest arrogance and hypocritical
humility. I chose the former and have seen no reason to change.*
—*Frank Lloyd Wright*

Frank Lloyd Wright's ascension from a Wisconsin farm boy to one of the most famous architects in the United States was certainly an unwavering one. His parents' marriage may have been based more on expediency than love, and the nomadic life into which he was born could not have been conducive to becoming a man who would redefine how American families would live: in homes designed to bring families together rather than keep them apart.

After their son, who was named Frank Lincoln Wright, was born, the family moved a few miles south to the town of Spring Green, Wisconsin. Anna was thrilled she had had a son, whom she determined would be a great architect, and to inspire him, she hung pictures of European cathedrals around his crib. These pictures were Wright's first introduction to the world of architecture.

In 1869, the family was on the move again, this time to McGregor, Iowa, where the townspeople welcomed William Wright as their new Baptist minister. In McGregor, Anna delivered her second child, a girl named Mary Jane. McGregor is on the east side of the Mississippi River. The founders had situated their port town harbor just north of the confluence of the Wisconsin and Mississippi Rivers. McGregor was over fifty miles from Anna's family. However, by 1857, the Milwaukee & Mississippi Railway had extended its tracks to Prairie du Chien, Wisconsin, from Madison. Prairie du Chien had been founded on the opposite side of the Mississippi River from McGregor, and both towns had become thriving transportation hubs for passengers, goods, and agricultural products. This rail line made it possible for Anna to return home and see her family.

The Wrights' next move came in 1871 and took them across the country to the city of Pawtucket, Rhode Island, where William had been offered the pastor's position at the High Street Baptist Church. This move was over 1,100 miles from the homelands of Anna's extended family.

William must have thought this was going to be a good decision for himself and his family because he was moving back to the area of the country where he had grown up. However, money troubles still plagued him and his church, and in 1875, he had to relinquish his position. Not only had he given up his job, but he lost his home at the parsonage, too. With little money and no steady job prospects, William sought refuge in the home of his father, who was now living in Weymouth, Massachusetts. Anna had little interest in staying in Weymouth, but the family could not finance another move across the country. Nevertheless, by living in Weymouth, the family could afford the thirty-minute train ride to Boston, and from Boston, there were trains heading to every major city east of the Mississippi River. The family's access to these trains coupled with the time they were in Weymouth provided Frank Lloyd Wright with a watershed moment in his life because in 1876, the city of Philadelphia hosted the Centennial International Exhibition, which celebrated the signing of the Declaration of Independence. Among the national and international displays, Switzerland had built a Swiss chalet to showcase the country's industries, its culture, and the staples of family life in this landlocked European nation. There, in addition to exhibits of Swiss watches, artfully crafted music boxes, and clocks that would announce the hour with birdsongs, Anna found a demonstration of the early childhood educational system developed by the German educator Friedrich Froebel. Froebel's educational system used hands-on play and outdoor work in the garden to expand a child's world by giving them the experience of lesson plans with tactile activities rather than being confined to a desk with a schoolmarm narrating information from a book.

Froebel began his work in Germany, but his ideas on education, especially the early education of young children, had migrated out of Germany and across Europe. Froebel had lived in Switzerland for a time, where he opened schools and shared his teaching ideas, which were readily adopted. The presentation that Anna saw included educational items like books and examples of assignments completed by Swiss schoolchildren. Also on display were articles that explained the methods of playing with different "gifts." These gifts, which were created by Frobel, included sets of blocks, shapes made from paper, strings, and small balls. The gifts were stored in wooden boxes that were originally numbered from one through six. In Froebel's system, each lesson learned was applied to the next lesson to continually build knowledge. Anna found the information on Frobel's system fascinating, and she knew she had to learn more about this unique system, and she needed to share these ideas with her son.

Domestic life for the Wright family was also changing. In Weymouth, the last of William and Anna's children—Margaret Ellen, known as Maginel—was born. The marriage between Anna and William began to grow tiresome for Anna, and she missed her family back in Wisconsin. However, she was able to arrange for extended vacations for herself and "her children" back in Wisconsin. Anna may have rekindled her independent spirit on one of these trips. By 1878, the tension in the Wrights' home was wearing on the family, and to appease Anna, William agreed to move back to Wisconsin. Once there, William acquired a home in Madison, changed religious affiliations, and accepted the position of pastor at the Liberal Unitarian Church in the small village of Wyoming, Wisconsin. Anna's family may have helped with placement.

Back in her home state and with her own three children to raise, being the stepmother to Permelia's three children was something Anna no longer had interest in or time for. Of all her stepchildren, Anna held the greatest disdain for young Elizabeth Amelia, who was every bit her mother's daughter and looked just like her. And as much as Anna revered her boy Frank, William adored Elizabeth.

Madison was some forty miles southeast of Spring Green, but Anna felt like she was back in the valley near her family once again. Now back in the safety of her Wisconsin homeland and within the protective realm of her large Welsh family, she needed a husband less and less.

Anna was becoming increasingly negative toward William and his children. William's children, Charles, George, and Elizabeth, were a source of utter aggravation to her, and she treated the children poorly and even wickedly at times. The stories of Anna's mistreatment were eventually shared with Permelia's mother, and she was appalled at Anna's behavior. Regardless of any objections from William, she collected her grandchildren and found new homes for the three siblings with Permelia's brothers and sisters.

It seems that William did not protest this idea, as he was probably afraid of losing another wife if he did. Even with William's children gone, the marriage continued to decline. In 1885, William filed for divorce; Anna did not protest, and the divorce became final in April that year. William Wright left his wife and his remaining three children. After William left his son, Frank had no contact with him again.

Anna's favorite son was now eighteen years old and had little affinity for his father, while on the other hand, he was extremely close to his mother and her family. To show his support for his mother and to show how he was

Lloyd Jones family photo (1883). *Back row, third and fourth from right*: Anna and William Wright. *Second row, third from right (with young girl on lap)*: Frank Lloyd Wright. *Image Reproduction & Licensing Wisconsin Historical Society.*

becoming an independent man, he dropped the middle name Lincoln and supplanted the name Lloyd in its place.

As the Wright family traveled from one state to another, young Frank grew up with an ever-changing form of education at the various public schools in the different towns where his family lived. But he was also exposed to the wonders of nature on his uncle's farms in southern Wisconsin. He was tutored by his mother in Frobel's educational system, where he had his first lesson in geometry and construction. Wright rarely spoke of his father, but William did provide his son with an education in classical music. His father would play the works of Beethoven for the family to enjoy. As time went on, Wright would also come to enjoy the compositions of other classical music composers such as Johann Sebastian Bach, Wolfgang Amadeus Mozart, and Johannes Brahms. With his father's guidance, he learned to play Beethoven's symphonies, sonatas, and concertos on the piano; all of these would stay with him for his entire life.

By 1875, the State of Wisconsin had set up eighteen free high schools, one of which was in Madison near where Wright and his family were living. As a teenager, Frank would have gone to this school. Wright did not graduate from high school; instead, he began working for a friend of his mother's, a civil engineer named Dr. Allen D. Conover who was also a professor at the University of Wisconsin and had recently opened private practice in Madison, where he allowed young Frank to work as a clerk or office boy. During the time Wright was working at Conover's office, Conover was appointed by the university to supervise the construction of the new Science Hall building. This building still stands on the university's Madison campus. This would have been Wright's first opportunity to be on an actual construction site in a professional capacity as a paid employee. Wright would have been assigned the duties of a clerk for Conover's firm, running errands, cleaning up the office, and occasionally sitting in on the discussions about the various projects that were being worked on. Wright was not afraid of self-promotion even though he was still a teenager; as soon as he had the chance, he added his name and his (assumed) position with Dr. Conover's firm to the Madison-area address book. On page 204 of the 1886 edition of the Madison, Wisconsin city directory, we find an entry for Anna Wright's residence, which was at 804 East Gorham, and two lines below that, we see that a second person was using that address as his residence, as well. The name we see there is "Wright Frank L. draughtsman A.D. Conover, res 804 E. Gorham."

Wright's position may have included carrying instructions from the office to the Science Hall building's work crews. We can only assume that with Wright's bravado, he provided these messages as if they had come from himself.

Having not graduated high school, Wright would not have met the minimum requirements to attend the University of Wisconsin. But with help from Dr. Conover, he was able to enroll as a "Special Student." It must not have been uncommon for the administration to allow students into the university with this designation, as Wright was one of four students granted this privilege in 1885. Wright is on a roster of students who were "Present During the Latter Part of 1885–1886." According to Wright's admissions cards, which were found in the university's archives, Wright registered for two classes in the fall of 1885: Solid Geometry and Descriptive Geometry.

For the spring semester, Wright registered for another two classes, trigonometry and a second geometry class.

In Wright's autobiography, he often refers to himself in the third person. When discussing his "years" in college, he writes the following:

> *In love with the grand gestures and in common with the others—he got himself a mortarboard with a beautiful red silk tassel hanging overboard.*

Joesph Lyman Silsbee. *Courtesy of Christopher Payne.*

Wright would have us believe that he graduated from the university; why else would he have needed a mortarboard with a red tassel? The choice of a red tassel is curious, because the School of Engineering, in which Wright was enrolled, would have required a yellow tassel on graduation, not red. Of course, how would he have known that, having not graduated at all? The two classes in the fall of 1886 were to be the last of his university career. Frank Lloyd Wright left the University of Wisconsin without receiving a diploma. However, during his lifetime, he went on to receive seven honorary degrees from various colleges and universities, including the University of Wisconsin.

With his formal education being limited, Wright had a second opportunity to receive architectural training in 1886, provided through the firm of Joseph Lyman Silsbee. Wright's uncle (on his mother's side of the family) was the Reverend Jenkin Lloyd Jones, a Unitarian minister. He persuaded Silsbee to leave Syracuse, New York, and come to the Midwest. Reverend Jones must have known of Silsbee's work, and he wanted him to design a chapel for the Lloyd-Jones family in Spring Green, Wisconsin. He was also planning a new church building for his own congregation in Chicago, and he wanted Silsbee to be the architect. This church became known as All Souls, and it was located on Chicago's south side on Cottage Grove Avenue.

Silsbee had had a successful career working in both Syracuse and Buffalo, New York, before moving to Chicago. Silsbee agreed to the move but must have thought his prospects for more work were better in Chicago than Madison or Milwaukee, because that is where he opened his new office. Within months, Wright would be heading to Chicago himself, and once there, he would find a position at Silsbee's firm. It was here, under the more temperate Silsbee, that Wright's independent work was first launched.

Much has been made of the influence Louis Sullivan's ideas had on Wright, but Silsbee, an accomplished architect in his own right, made an impression on Wright also, even though Wright's tenure in Silsbee's office lasted only months, rather than years. Wright was exposed to Silsbee's architectural designs, and he saw firsthand how to manage the business side of the firm.

1886 TO 1887

Apprenticeship with Joseph Lyman Silsbee

Silsbee could draw with amazing ease. He drew with soft, deep black lead-pencil strokes and he would make remarkable free-hand sketches of that type of dwelling peculiarly his own at the time.
—Frank Lloyd Wright

Unity Chapel, Spring Green, Wisconsin

In 1886, Wright had the privilege of working on a small family church that his uncle the Reverend Jenkin Lloyd Jones had contracted with Joseph Lyman Silsbee to design. It was noted by William C. Gannett, a friend of Reverend Jones's, in an article about the Lloyd-Jones family chapel in the August 1886 issue of the All Souls Church bulletin that "the interiors were looked after by a boy architect belonging to the family."

This "boy architect" has always been assumed to have been Frank Lloyd Wright. Even though Wright was nineteen years old in 1886, he had a childish face, and though he claimed to be taller, even with shoes on he only stood five feet, seven inches, thus looking more like a boy than a young man.

The location of the church was in Helena Valley on the Wisconsin River, the paternal land of the Lloyd-Jones family. The church, which still stands today, has a strong stone base. The wood-frame building is shaped as a shallow *L*; it is a shingled structure, which was a common design element for Silsbee's buildings. If you were riding by the church, you might even mistake it for a lovely home nestled in the valley. The interior has a fireplace and large open areas on either side. There is a belfry with a cast bell. The front entrance is reached by ascending four small steps to enter a covered porch; there are two sets of three double-hung windows on the wall opposite the entry. To the left of the doorway is a single double-hung window, with a corresponding matching window on the opposite side of the room. Even though the church is plain, it has stood the test of time and is still used for some church services today.

The circumstances surrounding Wright's departure from Madison and his arrival in Chicago are hazy at best; the only written account of the adventure is from Wright himself. He gives a short account of his arrival in Chicago in his autobiography. Wright tells us that he found himself at

Unity Chapel, Spring Green, Wisconsin (1959). *Image Reproduction & Licensing Wisconsin Historical Society.*

the Wells Street train station in the spring of 1886. This was one of the stations on the Chicago and Northwestern railway line, which was extended to Madison from Chicago. On his arrival, Wright took a room in the Briggs Hotel, which was about five blocks south of Wells Street Station. He set out the next morning in search of a job. In his autobiography, he writes that he searched the city for an opportunity—any opportunity—to begin working at one of the city's many architectural firms. Alas, he did not receive any offers, and within days, he was rationing what little money he had and cautiously selecting meals that would be filling but inexpensive. At the finer hotels in Chicago, room rates could range from $3.50 to $7.00. Assuming Wright initially opted for a less expensive room, he was soon asking the hotel clerk for an even lower-priced room. According to Wright's autobiography, a clerk offered him a room for $0.75 a night, which he was grateful for, and he thought it was just as agreeable as his original room.

Wright did not want to lean on his uncle Jenkin's name to get a job; in fact, his uncle had cautioned Wright's mother against allowing the boy to come to Chicago at all.

Finally, Wright put his pride in his pocket and tried Silsbee's office. Eureka—he landed his first job in Chicago.

In Wright's autobiography, his narrative borrows the theme of a Horatio Alger dime novel: the poor boy who struggles against all odds becomes a classic American success story. It has been said that Wright's greatest creation was the story of his own life, and this idea of coming to the big city alone with nowhere to go and barely any money just may have been his way of positioning himself on the bottom rung of life's ladder. What is more plausible is that Wright headed for Chicago knowing that his uncle Jenkin had retained Silsbee to design the new church for his All Souls congregation and hoping he could land a job by using his uncle's relationship with Silsbee.

The type of church building Reverend Jones wanted would not be a simple country church. This building would have stature and a commanding presence in an urban location. It would not be a Gothic building nor a church with steeples and large stained-glass windows; this building would not only be a church, but it would also be Jenkin Lloyd Jones's home. There would be classrooms for the education of the parishioners' children and even a place for social activities. All would be welcome in this house of God. Jenkin had always intended the building to resemble a house; he believed God's house should be a place where the members of his flock could find peace and contentment as they worshiped or took part in communal gatherings. This was one of the main reasons Jenkin sought out Silsbee; the broad, shingle-style Queen Anne homes he had designed were a model for what All Souls Church would become. There were moments in Wright's life when his timing was impeccable, and his lonely trip to Chicago in hopes of beginning his architectural career was well gauged to coincide with the period of his uncle's connection with Silsbee as they designed and built Reverend Jones's new church.

In Maginel Wright's biography of the Lloyd-Jones family, written in 1965, she supports Wright's version of his trek to Chicago in hopes of finding a job. But she had only two sources to consult: her brother's autobiography, originally written in 1932, and any comments she may have heard from her brother.

When Wright appeared at Silsbee's office, he was met by a young draftsman named Cecil Corwin. Frank and Cecil became close friends, but Wright also befriended two other draftsmen who worked at Silsbee's office, George W. Maher and George G. Elmslie. All four of these men would become Prairie-style architects.

Wright's job at Silsbee's office was that of a tracer, a position that paid eight dollars a week. In 1886, that salary had significant buying power. In the late 1880s, regular, daily household items cost about five dollars a week. For

Left: Frank Lloyd Wright.
Right: Cecil Corwin.
Courtesy of Douglas M. Steiner, Edmonds, WA.

Frank Lloyd Wright this meant he could buy an expertly tailored suit of fine European cloth for under ten dollars after tailoring. A theater ticket could cost as little fifty cents, or one dollar for the reserved seats on the first floor, and a meal with all the trimmings at the Berghoff Restaurant, which opened in 1898, could be had for less than one dollar.

Wright's salary of eight dollars a week suited him well, at least for a while.

J.L. Cochrane Edgewater Subdivision, Lakeview, Illinois

During the time that Wright worked in Silsbee's office, the firm was contracted to design homes for a housing complex for a prominent Chicago real estate developer named J.L. Cochrane. The project was in a subdivision called Edgewater. The Edgewater neighborhood was part of the city of Lakeview, which was just north of the Chicago city limits. In 1889, Lakeview and the Edgewater community would be annexed into the city of Chicago.

The area is bounded by Lake Michigan to the east, and it was this proximity to the lakefront that made the area ripe for development. Cochrane's advertisement gave prospective home buyers the enticement of living in an idyllic new housing development. He encouraged home buyers to see what made Edgewater different, citing the "Edgewater Way." People read about how the streets were already paved, the sewer and water supply lines were

J.L. Cochrane subdivision advertisement. *Chicago History Museum, ICHi-037108.*

already in the ground, and streets and homes had electric lights installed. Joseph Lyman Silsbee drew a perspective of Cochrane's personal home, which would be built in Edgewater. The architect's drawing clearly tells us that Silsbee is the architect of record; however, a second signature is also legible on the drawing, the monogram of Frank Lloyd Wright as the delineator of the design. Wright had outgrown his position as a tracer, and by 1887, he was working as a delineator. His tasks would have been to complete formal drawings of various projects. The architect may have drawn the building, but the delineator made it come alive by creating presentation drawings that would include foliage on the ground and clouds in the sky. The best drawing would be used for demonstrations to prospective clients. In Cochrane's newspaper advertisement, which included the drawing of his new home, Silsbee's signature was cut off. However, the young delineator's autograph is visible just to the left of center. Briefly, one might have thought the signature was that of the architect since it was the only one in view.

Though it is difficult to read in this advertisement from 1887, the signature is Wright's. During his tenure at Silsbee's office, the firm was busy; besides Cochrane's subdivision, it had received contracts for five individual residences and an office building for the Illinois Telephone and Telegraph Company. It is likely that Wright had the opportunity to work on these projects. It was also during this time that Wright began to seek out opportunities for his own commissions and to promote himself by submitting his work for publication.

Unitarian Chapel, Sioux City, Iowa

A project Wright had published in the *Inland Architect* journal in June 1887 was a design for a small Unitarian chapel for a congregation in Sioux City, Iowa. The actual design put forth by Wright and the building that was eventually built for the congregation bore little resemblance to each other. In fact, Wright's design has more similarities to Silsbee's Unity Chapel of 1886 than anything else.

When comparing the building designed by Wright and the chapel designed by Silsbee and built for the Lloyd-Jones family, several similarities can be noted. Both buildings include a strong stone foundation that rises from the ground to the windowsills. Silsbee's Unity Chapel has traditional double-hung windows, while Wright's chapel windows are a combination of leaded diamond panes on top and what look like sliding windows on the lower half. Wright would continue to design windows and glass doorways and cabinet doors with both stylized natural elements and/or geometric patterns throughout his career.

Silsbee's entryway is a wooden shingled porch that is covered by the building's roof and has a large open bay to the left. Wright's entry is also covered by a section of the roof, but the entrance is through a large Roman arch built of stone. Silsbee's chapel includes a belfry and cast bell, to call the family in from the field for services, while Wright's design excludes this feature. Unity Chapel is a small, wood-framed building shaped like an *L* and shrouded in wooden shingles. The Unitarian chapel in Wright's design is an oblong structure. There is a small alcove to one side and a place for either the pastor's office or study across the room. The Spring Green chapel has a fireplace and chimney internal to the building, and Wright's design includes a fireplace, as well. Wright drew a decorative bar that would have provided support for the chimney from the adjacent roof. The design of the decoration was that of a leafy vine. One feature Wright included that Silsbee did not is a large conical tower that extends several feet above the main roofline.

Wright submitted his chapel design for publication to the *Inland Architect*, and it was published in June 1887. His name and his profession as an "architect" are included in the list of other illustrators whose work was published in that month's journal. The *Inland Architect* had staunch support among architects in Chicago and beyond. Several prominent architects contributed articles to the June issue, including Daniel Burnham, William Lebron Jenney, John Root, and Louis Sullivan. Joseph Lyman Silsbee did not supply any articles or illustrations for the June edition, but he was a

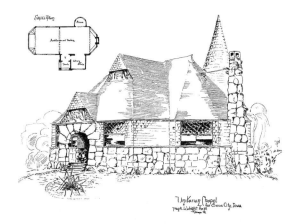

Unitarian chapel, Sioux City, Iowa. *Chicago History Museum, ICHi-182710.*

regular contributor and served on several local and national committees whose activities were reported on in this monthly journal. There is no doubt Silsbee would have seen Wright's published drawing. Was this the start of Wright's moonlighting career?

The curious thing about the Unitarian chapel commission is that there is no known communication between Wright and the Sioux City congregation asking for a design. The church building that was eventually constructed for the congregation was built to hold three hundred parishioners. The design for this church was prepared by an architect named J.W. Martin in 1888, and the dedication of the completed church building was held on May 5, 1889. The *Sioux City Journal* reported on the dedication services in its morning edition on May 7, 1889. The article mentions Mr. Martin's design and the fact that Reverend Jenkin Lloyd Jones delivered a sermon to celebrate the dedication. What likely happened is that Wright, having become aware of the congregation's plans for a new church from his uncle, saw an opportunity to execute a drawing and have it published under his own name to announce to the world that Frank Lloyd Wright, architect, had landed in Chicago and was ready to take on all projects—and soon after this publication, he got the call for his first executed building.

Hillside Home School, Spring Green, Wisconsin

Two of Frank Lloyd Wright's aunts on his mother's side, Jane and Ellen Lloyd Jones, were educators, just as Wright's mother had been. These sisters never married, and when their parents passed, they inherited the family

Hillside Home School. *Courtesy of Douglas M. Steiner, Edmonds, WA.*

farm. The sisters were so close that the family referred to them both as "the Aunts." The two spinsters decided to build and run a boarding school on the farm that had been bequeathed to them. They contacted their nephew in Chicago and asked him to design the first building for their new school. Wright must have been delighted to perform this service for his Aunts. The building became known as the Hillside Home School.

THE SCHOOL WAS DESIGNED by Wright while he was working in Silsbee's office. Therefore, it is quite plausible that even though this building is credited as Wright's first built commission, Silsbee oversaw his young draftsman's work. The building, which stood for over fifty years, had three floors, including separate boarding rooms for both boys and girls; classrooms; a kitchen; and a dining room. The exterior of the building was clad in wood, like Silsbee's shingle-style Queen Anne homes. The entry included a large, rounded arch, and there was a shaded porch that fronted the building. The roof was a standard gabled one. There were also gutters and downspouts, elements that Wright would eventually remove for his Prairie homes. The exteriors of the first and second floors were delineated by two horizontal bands of wood that were spaced about twelve feet apart. The lower band traveled the full width of the building and then wrapped around to the back of the building. The upper band did not transverse the porch's upper veranda but began at a point just after it. This band became the lower sill for the second-floor windows. When the building was completed, the boarding school opened in 1887, and the Aunts operated their private school until 1915. Wright eventually bought the site from his Aunts. After Wright purchased the land and building, he had his first built commission torn down to make room for his beloved Taliesin.

Helena Valley Residence No. 1, Spring Green, Wisconsin

The next two drawings Wright created while working for Silsbee were also published in the *Inland Architect*. Wright created two building designs that he listed as being residences for Helena Valley, in Wisconsin. The area Wright was referring to is the valley where his maternal family had settled. The town of Helena, Wisconsin, was once found close to this area. To ensure the economic survival of their town, the residents of Helena moved their little hamlet twice, finally settling near the Milwaukee and Mississippi Railroad train line, which had laid tracks from Milwaukee toward Madison. Today, Helena is no more than an unincorporated dot on the Wisconsin state map, near the Wisconsin & Southern Railroad.

The first of Wright's two home designs appeared in the August 1887 issue of the journal. The second home design appeared in the February 1888 edition. The buildings represented by these drawings were not executed. Wright again had his work published for the sake of having his name and abilities shown off to his colleagues. We do not find Wright's contemporaries such as Cecil Corwin or George Elmslie publishing drawings in these pages, just the ever-ambitious Frank Lloyd Wright. George Maher had a design for a home published in the August 1888 issue of the journal, but by then, he had left Silsbee's firm and started his own practice.

The first drawing, from August 1887, is for a "Country Residence for Hillside Estate Helena Valley Wisconsin," drawn by "F.L. Wright Architect Chicago, IL." Ten different firms had drawings published in this issue; four were on full pages, and the remaining six each shared half a page with another drawing. Wright's illustration is on the top half of the third page of sketches published.

Country Residence for Hillside Estate Helena Valley, no. 1. *Chicago History Museum, ICHi-182712.*

The home has a large veranda, which is seen from the front elevation, and it has an arcade of arches traversing this expanse. The exterior is not clad in shingles; for this project, Wright used wood lapped siding. A gable roof is employed on this three-story building. The windows on the second floor are shown with grills or mullions. Up to this point, each of Wright's published drawings had been reduced to half a page and the page shared with another illustrator.

Helena Valley Residence No. 2, Spring Green, Wisconsin

As noted previously, the next design for a home in the "Valley" was published in the February 1888 issue of the *Inland Architect*. This design is given a full page to show two perspectives of the same building. Wright's drawing shows a home that includes many of the same features seen in the Hillside Home School building.

The location of the project, Wright's name, and his chosen profession are clearly printed on the bottom of the page. The February 1888 issue included eight submittals from other architects. Each presenter added their own style for titling their work. Two presenters added a fanciful three-part banner for the titles of their drawings, while the others' titles, including Wright's, were much more understated.

Some authors have characterized these early drawings as those of a novice designer, even to the point of dismissing them as possibly being incompetent copies of others' work. These comments infer that the drawings are from the hand of an amateur, but that is, in fact, what Wright was at that time. The more important facts are that he was submitting his work for publication in a recognized professional journal and that he was labeling himself as an architect, even though he was only employed as a competent delineator or

Country Residence for Hillside Estate Helena Valley, no 2. *Chicago History Museum, ICHi-182711.*

possibly a draftsman. This shows that even in the earliest part of his career, he was enhancing his reputation and completed work on his own outside of the firm he was working for.

It is likely that this last drawing was published after Wright left Silsbee's firm to begin working for Adler & Sullivan; however, this was not the first time he had left Silsbee's firm. By the fall of 1887, Frank Lloyd Wright was looking for a higher salary, but Silsbee was not willing to pay him any more than the twelve dollars a week he had recently raised his salary to. If others in Silsbee's office were making do on salaries between eight and twelve dollars a week, that was no match for Wright's spending habits.

In his autobiography, Wright recounts his conversation with Silsbee when he asked for a second salary increase in 1887.

Wright: "Mr. Silsbee, I can't get along on twelve dollars a week. Don't you think I can earn fifteen dollars at least—now?"

Silsbee: "You've just had a raise, Wright. No! Perhaps—after the first of the year."

Wright: "I quit."

This story not only gives us an example of how impetuous and quick-tongued Wright could be—but as this story continues, we will also see how he could work his way out of a problem he himself created.

After walking out on Silsbee, Wright tells us, he went to see the architect W.W. Clay for a position. When Clay asked him what salary he expected, Wright told him eighteen dollars a week. He must have thought he would end up at fifteen dollars a week after negotiating. Clay agreed to the eighteen dollars and set Wright to work. Wright soon found himself in a bit of a quandary, and in a rare moment of self-reflection, Wright realized the work he was being assigned was beyond his capabilities. However, he convinced himself that there was no one in Clay's firm that would be able to teach him anything more than what he already knew. Wright shared his difficulties with Mr. Clay, and in the ensuing conversation, Wright told him he was leaving and going back to Silsbee's firm, with only the hope that he could get his old job back.

For Wright, this move turned out better than he could have wished for. Not only did Silsbee allow his wayward employee to come back, but he also agreed to pay him the same wages Clay had offered him. In a matter of weeks instead of months, Wright was able to raise his salary by over 60 percent.

Sometime late in the year 1887 or early 1888, Wright heard that Adler & Sullivan were adding staff, and he saw his chance to move to one of the most prestigious firms in Chicago.

Chapter 1

1888: Frank Lloyd Wright
Joins the Firm of His Mentor

His own beautiful drawings…are better testimony
than any I could offer in words.
—*Frank Lloyd Wright, writing about Louis Sullivan*

A s we begin the discussion of Wright's time at Adler & Sullivan, I will
share with you the criteria I used to determine whether a building can
be considered a bootleg design or not.

The first deciding factor would be the period of the commission. Wright's
ability to work independently most likely did not begin until 1892, and he
left Adler & Sullivan's firm sometime in 1893. Therefore, any commission
completed before 1892 or after 1893 would not be a bootleg design.

A bootleg design must have an actual client present. It is disputed
whether a client relationship existed for one of the projects we will be
reviewing. If there is no actual client, the project should not be considered
a bootleg commission.

How Wright received a commission must be determined, if possible. Did
the project come through the firm? Or did the client seek out Wright on
their own?

When and where did Wright complete the drawings for the building? Any
work Wright did in the office would most certainly have been work assigned
by the firm. His bootleg commissions were drawn up in his home studio in
Oak Park.

Was there an effort by Wright to conceal his involvement in the design of a particular commission? If there was, then the project would have been a bootleg design.

The final criteria would be: Did the commission result in a completed house? If not, then the project cannot be considered a bootleg house.

It may not be necessary for all these points to be true, but there should be enough evidence established by using these categories to determine any building's lineage during Wright's bootleg phase.

Frank Lloyd Wright writes in his autobiography that a man named Wilcox told him that Adler & Sullivan were hiring. It seems that Wilcox had interviewed at the firm himself but did not receive an offer. However, according to Wright's recollection, Wilcox told Sullivan about Wright and paved the way for him. Wright, not wanting to waste a moment, pulled together drawings from his desk and quickly set off to see Louis H. Sullivan.

Wright did indeed interview with Sullivan, and he saved one of the drawings he brought in for Sullivan to review. The drawing's catalog number is 8701. The drawing itself has an interesting history, one that was quite important to Wright.

Wright added handwritten notes to the drawing that obscure its lineage. In the lower right-hand corner, there is an undated note that says: "Study Drawing House made in Madison previous to going to Chicago." Wright is telling the world he did this drawing before arriving in Chicago. Could this be true? He also gives us a clue about the first time the drawing became a presentation piece. In the lower left-hand corner, he added the following notation: "Drawing Home to Lieber Meister when angling for a job."

Wright may have brought more than one drawing to the interview, but he only saved this one. This drawing was so important to Wright that it was one of the first drawings shown in an exhibit of Wright's life's work that was held at the Museum of Modern Art in 2017: *Frank Lloyd Wright at 50: Unpacking the Archive.*

With this drawing, we are faced with our first ambiguity about the date of one of Wright's recorded sketches. According to Wright's biography, he arrived in Chicago in 1886. How could he have created this drawing in Madison, before going to Chicago and before he even would have known he would be having a job interview with the man who would be his mentor?

Wright may have had this drawing safely tucked into his briefcase and ready to present when the need arose. He must have felt the drawing was a good representation of his independent work. And it's quite possible that Wright returned to Madison at some point to visit with his mother and sisters, who were still living in Wisconsin at that time, where he could have created this drawing hoping to secure an interview with another firm and only added the notes about "made in Madison" or "angling for a job" later.

Another interesting fact about this plan sheet is that there is another comment written on the page that reads: "Project Cooper House, La Grange, Ill." However, someone has scribbled over those words, as if to strike them off the page. Any specific comments Louis Sullivan may have made about Wright's drawings did not find their way into print. According to Wright's autobiography, Sullivan only said: "These aren't the kinds of drawings I'd like to see.…Make some drawings of ornament or ornamental details and bring them back, I want to look at them."

Sullivan's purpose in requesting these types of drawings must have been to see if this young draftsman, who had only been working in Chicago for a brief time, could prepare suitable reproductions of Sullivan's ideas and designs to create the working drawings for the artisans and mold makers who would be completing the adornments Sullivan was to create for the interiors of the Auditorium Theater Building.

At their second meeting, Sullivan must have found Wright's work satisfactory, because Wright began working for Adler & Sullivan in the early months of 1888. Originally, he was just one of the draftsmen working for hourly wages at the firm. Wright and Sullivan were to become quite a duo, with Sullivan as the master and Wright the apprentice. Wright got on so well at the firm that in 1889, he requested some form of job security, and he was offered a five-year employment contract. Wright had another inducement to nailing down a contracted position with his firm: his soon-to-be in-laws would be much more accepting of the marriage of their eldest daughter to this young man when his position at the firm he was working for was secure.

Within days of signing his employment contract, Wright then asked for a loan of $5,000 from the firm to buy a vacant lot and fund the construction of a home for himself and Catherine Lee Tobin, his bride-to-be. Wright would have regular withdrawals taken out of his weekly salary to extinguish the mortgage loan. Believing their future and their finances were settled, Frank and Catherine would settle down and raise their family in the quiet Chicago suburb of Oak Park, Illinois.

In Wright's autobiography, he claims that after he arrived at Adler & Sullivan's firm, the principals kept busy with designing commercial buildings and any residential work was given to Wright to work out on his own. These residential commissions were often for former clients or friends of the firm. One of first buildings whose design shows Wright's work was the three-door townhouse for Victor Faulkner. This building was erected on Wabash Avenue in Chicago (1888). Wright had completed a fair amount of work up to this point, including summer homes for both Louis Sullivan and his neighbor James Charnley in Ocean Springs, Mississippi (1891). Wright claimed that he also designed the Albert Sullivan house (1892) and the Charnleys' Chicago home (1892). He also designed two commercial projects for the firm: the first was a four-story apartment building (1892), and the second was the Victoria Hotel, which was erected in Chicago Heights, Illinois (1893). All these commissions except the apartment building and the Victoria Hotel are listed both in the roster of buildings designed by the firm of Adler & Sullivan and in the Wright archives. The firm gave Wright the opportunity to work on some of these commission in his off hours, at his home studio; he could then count the hours worked against the monthly mortgage fees for his loan in lieu of his salary. It was a mutually beneficial arrangement. However, for Wright, his interpretation of this agreement set him on a path that changed the course of his career.

The field of architecture looked down on the practice of moonlighting even before the American Institute of Architects came into existence in 1857. By 1888, the practice of moonlighting had become so prevalent and was thought to be so egregious that the Illinois Association of Architects was considering a change in its by-laws that would require the "expulsion" of any member for taking part in moonlighting.

In Wright's employment contract, there would surely have been a clause prohibiting moonlighting. But by 1892, Wright was supplementing his income with proceeds from residential home designs that had been contracted not through his firm but through his own volition.

Wright was no stranger to stepping outside the confines of the firm he was working for and passing himself off as an independent architect. As noted earlier, when Wright was employed at Joseph Lyman Silsbee's firm, he had three renderings submitted for publication in the *Inland Architect*, naming himself as the architect, with no mention of Silsbee's firm. None of these three projects became bona fide commissions, and it is quite possible the intended clients were only created as a convenience for Wright.

As the year 1889 began, it set off a busy time for Wright: it was the year he not only married his first love, Catherine Tobin, but also designed his own home. It is during 1890 that we see Wright coming upon one of the detours he will face in his career, when he begins to work from home on the firm's projects. If he continues to do this type of work, both the firm and he himself will prosper. But is this what he wants to do—be Sullivan's understudy? Could Wright have begun to wonder: If he was working at home anyway, should it matter to the client whom they were paying their fees to?

Wright must have believed that it would not.

After the success of the Auditorium Theater building, Adler & Sullivan's primary focus was on tall buildings and larger and more complex commissions. Wright was willingly taking on the firm's residential work. He may have had either Adler or Sullivan review the work, but by 1892, he was able to work on most projects independently.

The building design recorded as number 9002 in Wright's archives is for a residential home in Chicago for a friend of the Adler & Sullivan firm. The client's name was William S. MacHarg. Mr. MacHarg was an engineer who specialized in commercial and industrial plumbing, and he had been a consultant on many of the projects completed by Adler & Sullivan. The home was located on Beacon Street in Chicago. It has been hypothesized that this home was Wright's first bootleg commission. However, as the history of this commission becomes known, it seems unlikely that this could be true.

Chapter 2
1891 to 1893:
Frank Lloyd Wright's Bootleg Phase

THE CHICAGO HOMES

Eventually, I think Chicago will be the most beautiful great city
left in the world.
—*Frank Lloyd Wright*

Between 1891 and 1892, there were four residences designed and built in Chicago, Illinois, that have been linked to Wright's bootleg phase. The first home was from 1891 and was in the Sheridan Park area of the Uptown neighborhood, which had been annexed by the city of Chicago in 1889. Sheridan Park is located about six miles north of downtown Chicago.

Wright designed three more homes in 1892, and two of them were on neighboring lots in the Kenwood neighborhood. The fourth was constructed in North Kenwood. These two areas are about six miles southeast of downtown. Kenwood and North Kenwood were not separate villages; they were originally neighborhoods within the Hyde Park Township. The North Kenwood neighborhood was annexed into Chicago in 1893. Hyde Park Township, including Kenwood, had been annexed by the city of Chicago in 1889.

Berry/MacHarg House

Chicago, Illinois, 1891
Demolished 1926

The Berry/MacHarg house of 1891 is quite a curious project in the timeline of the bootleg homes. This house was a residential commission that has been attributed to both the firm of Adler & Sullivan and to Frank Lloyd Wright as an independent commission. If this were true, this commission could be considered Wright's first bootleg home. In Wright's archives, the number 9002 is assigned to this commission, while the catalog of works by Adler & Sullivan identifies the building as number 146.

Written documentation about the origins of the contract for this house has been lost to history. Any available construction documents or blueprints for the home have not been found, and there seems to be only one known photograph of the building in existence. There is also debate as to which family lived in the house first, that of Charles Berry or William MacHarg. A summary of the two men's time in Chicago may shed some light on this question.

Charles Berry was born in Mahopac, New York, in 1842. In 1864, he began his college career at the University of Michigan. Four years later, he graduated from the university's Medical College. After graduating, he moved to Chicago.

In the 1868 Lakeside directory for the city of Chicago, J.G. Brooks is listed as being in partnership with Mary Code in a dry goods business at 787 West Madison Avenue. However, one year later, the directory lists the partners of the same store as being Charles Berry and John D. Osgood. On Saturday, April 4, 1888, one of the first advertisements for medical services to be provided by a Dr. Hutchinson and Dr. Berry was published on page 18 of the *Chicago Tribune*, saying that for treatment of diseases "of the nose, throat, lungs, heart, stomach, liver, and kidneys," patients were encouraged to make their way to the "Chicago Dermal Institute located at 103 State Street, Doctor Hutchinson & Berry attending."

Charles H. Berry residence, Chicago, Illinois, 1891–92. Dankmar Adler and Louis H. Sullivan. *Richard Nickel Archive, Ryerson and Burnham Art and Architecture Archives, Art Institute of Chicago. Digital file #201006_110422-10.*

By 1889, Dr. Berry's newspaper advertisement no longer mentions Dr. Hutchinson, and his services changed to treatments for women's backaches and cures for skin diseases, catarrh, and nervous disorders. In 1890, we see that the advertisements for Dr. Berry's services fill the top half of an entire broadsheet page in the *Tribune*. These large ads start to mention that the good doctor treats the diseases listed previously, but he can also provide patients with an ointment that can remove freckles!

In 1898, Dr. Berry married Mary Mills, who was from Garret City, Indiana. On Dr. Berry's retirement, the couple moved back to Mary's hometown. In April 1902, Dr. Berry died after falling off his horse-drawn buggy when the buggy caught a wheel in a streetcar rail line in Garret City.

William MacHarg was born in 1847 in Albion, New York, and he also graduated from the University of Michigan in 1868. His degree was from the School of Mining. Three years after graduating, he married Francis Briggs, whom he met while he was at college. He moved to Chicago and began the MacHarg Plumbing Company.

MacHarg was so well respected in his field that Daniel Burnham appointed him to be the director of water, sewerage, gas, and fire protection for the 1893 World's Columbian Exhibition. MacHarg's name was continually mentioned in the local newspapers throughout his professional career for consulting on various engineering projects in the city of Chicago.

As listed in both the 1890 and 1891 Lakeside directories for Chicago, MacHarg's home address was 20 Chalmers Place; during these same two years, Dr. Berry was listed at the same address. Charles must have begun renting a room from MacHarg.

The Chicago city directory of 1892 shows that William MacHarg and his wife were living at 3227 Beacon Street, the original address of the home in question; the same directory lists Charles H. Berry at 100 East State Street. However, the voter registration records for Chicago in 1892 show that both Charles Berry and William MacHarg used 3227 Beacon Street as their permanent address. This fact could be what has led to researchers' uncertainty as to who the original owner was.

The handwriting for each of the entries in these registers shows that these names were filled in by county election officials rather than the individuals who were being listed.

The voter rolls for the following years do not show this discrepancy, and both the census records and the Chicago directories show only the MacHargs living at the Beacon Street address from 1893 onward. The Beacon Street home was listed as William's address in his obituary after he died in May 1910.

Cook County voter registration rolls, 1892. *Illinois Regional Archives Depository—Ronald Williams Library, Northeastern Illinois University.*

In most catalogs listing the work of Adler & Sullivan and the commissions of Wright, this home is labeled as the MacHarg House; sometimes there will be a footnote about Dr. Charles Berry's involvement, but that is not always the case. Based on the two men's professions, we can assume they had the financial means to buy land and have a custom home built. There is some anecdotal evidence that Dr. Berry purchased the lot and then sold it to MacHarg, or it could be that Berry rented a room for a brief time after the home was built. However, for this discussion, the home will be designated as the MacHarg house.

EVIDENCE OF THE HOME BEING A BOOTLEG DESIGN

Comparing the one existing photograph of the MacHarg house to the early photos of Louis Sullivan's Ocean Springs cottage and to the shingle-style buildings associated with Wright's Silsbee period, similarities can be found.

The exteriors are clad in wood shingles, and the house has a porch that sits on a brick base. The first-floor windows that can be seen are double-hung windows, like those in Sullivan's Ocean Springs cottage. However, one of the second-floor windows is an open casement window. Frank Lloyd Wright, as well as other Chicago architects, would advance the idea of using casement windows to increase ventilation in the years to come. It was one of Wright's fellow architects, a man named Robert C. Spencer, who referred to double-hung windows as guillotines to show his distaste for them; Wright said, later in his career, that "even if I lost [the] client, I would insist on" casement windows. Wright used casement windows throughout both the Prairie period and his Usonian period, too.

The style of porch on the MacHarg home was not used by Adler & Sullivan prior to this point. The perimeter of the porch has what looks to be a spindle rail fence, and again, this element was not used in any other Adler & Sullivan home design of this period. The Adler & Sullivan home for Morris Selz, built in 1883, does have a smaller porch with a set of steps leading up to the home, but the railing that surrounds the porch has an open design, instead of spindles. All these features would have been known to Adler & Sullivan, but they were not employed on any of their other residential commissions. When reviewing the catalog of buildings through Adler & Sullivan's history, common elements will be seen. This is not meant to suggest that their buildings were copies of one another. Each building would have its own personality, but Adler & Sullivan had certain go-to components, depending on the period of the building. The arched doorway was a consistent design element for Sullivan throughout his career, not unlike the hearth and inglenook was a common element for Wright throughout his.

If one chooses to begin with the conclusion that Wright planned the MacHarg home exclusively on his own, evidence can be developed to support that idea. However, to really answer the question of who the designer was, both sides of the argument must be looked at.

EVIDENCE THE HOME WAS NOT A BOOTLEG DESIGN

William MacHarg was a person quite well known to the firm of Adler & Sullivan. The assumption that Dr. Berry may have only rented a room in the house gives some credence to the idea that he originally purchased the land prior to selling the property to MacHarg. It is also quite plausible that, since Berry and MacHarg had a relationship, if the original client was Dr. Charles Berry, he may have sought out MacHarg's recommendation for an architect when he was looking to have a home built.

It does not seem likely that if William MacHarg purchased a new house, Dankmar Adler or Louis Sullivan would not have known about it. All three men had articles published in the *Inland Architect*; in fact, at the February meeting of the Illinois State Association of Architects, William MacHarg had presented a report on home drainage systems. At the conclusion of Mr. MacHarg's presentation, Dankmar Adler recommended that the full written article should be printed in the next edition of the association's monthly journal, which it was.

Obviously, Chicago architects, engineers, and contractors were a tight-knit group. These men worked on the same projects and had worked together in different firms as partners or as subordinates; they volunteered together on various professional committees and consulted each other when necessary. When William MacHarg shared the news about his home purchase with his friends and associates, the obvious question among the architects of the group would have been: "Who designed it?" There is another point that must be raised here. As a person associated with professionals in the building construction arena, William MacHarg would have known about the problem of moonlighting. MacHarg may also have known that Wright worked at Adler & Sullivan's firm, and it does not seem plausible that MacHarg would be involved in buying a home designed by someone working outside of their contract.

If MacHarg had realized Wright was moonlighting, would he not have mentioned this to his associates at Adler & Sullivan? If so, it is likely that—based on Sullivan's reaction to finding out, years later, that Wright had been moonlighting—this would have been the first and only bootleg house. Wright might have been let go from the firm at that time rather than being confronted about these homes two years later.

A more likely scenario is that the contract for the home was procured through the firm and Wright was assigned to manage the design. He could have worked on these plans at home. Since there are no photographs of the home's interior or even of the other elevations, we can only wonder what other attributes the building may have had.

Therefore, based on the information presented here, this author does not believe that the MacHarg home should be counted in the roster of bootleg houses.

The next two homes that Wright completed on his own were for clients who were looking for custom homes in an upscale neighborhood. They wanted their homes to express to the world that they had arrived. These clients purchased neighboring lots in the affluent Kenwood neighborhood of Hyde Park. The neighborhood was important, but they also wanted their homes to be distinctive. Kenwood was home to an exclusive group of residents in the 1890s. The city's first millionaires built their mansions there. Among the wealthiest residents of this exclusive enclave were Martin Ryerson, who made his fortune from the lumber trade; Gustavus Swift, of the meatpacking industry; and Julius Rosenwald, who was one of the top administrators at Sears Roebuck and Company. Chicago's Kenwood neighborhood has been able to hold on to its mystique of being a selective community through the years with many famous and or important people having lived there, including Muhammad Ali and several distinguished faculty members of the University of Chicago.

The first of Wright's commissions for 1892 was numbered 9201, and the client was named George Blossom.

George Blossom Home

Kenwood, Illinois, 1892

George Blossom was born in Dubuque, Iowa, in 1854. His future wife, Carrie Boardman, was born in Fort Wayne, Indiana, in 1867. As a young man, George had the opportunity to work at a local insurance agency in Dubuque. By the time of the 1880 census, both George and Carrie were living in Chicago with their respective families. After moving to Chicago, George continued his career in the insurance industry when he began working for the firm of Fred S. James & Company.

In 1888, George and Carrie were married, and in 1890, their son George Jr. was born. In 1892, their second son, Frances, arrived, and in 1898, their only daughter, Katherine, was born.

The young couple's family was growing, and George was making a name for himself in the insurance industry as the assistant manager and agent for

George Blossom residence, Chicago, Illinois, 1892. Frank Lloyd Wright. *Historic Architecture and Image Collection Ryerson and Burnham Art and Architecture Archives, Art Institute of Chicago, #19785.*

the National of Hartford Insurance Agency. In 1894, an article in the *Chicago Tribune* listed Eugene Harback as the president of the newly reorganized Western Factory Association; his partner George Blossom was the secretary. This company was going to be supplying brokerage services for twenty different insurance companies. George's career had flourished in Chicago. He was a member of the Union League Club, which was founded in the mid-1800s to provide financial backing for Abraham Lincoln's efforts to preserve the Union. George was also a member of two different country clubs, and he and his wife's travel itineraries were often listed in the newspaper's society pages. George's opinions on business affairs were quoted in the local paper's financial sections, too.

The Blossoms' family connection to Frank Lloyd Wright came through mutual attendance at All Souls Church. In 1889, when George and Carrie were married, the Reverend Coleman Adams, a minister from All Souls, presided over their wedding.

Exactly why Wright chose to work on this commission by himself without using the firm's resources is unknown. However, for Wright, it was just the next step on his path to becoming an independent architect. This had been Wright's goal ever since he listed himself as a draftsman working for A.D. Conover in the 1884 edition of the local Madison, Wisconsin address book, even though he was nothing more than a clerk hired by Conover as a favor to his mother.

In 1892 Mr. Blossom found his name and his home's building plans printed in the monthly *Inland Architect*. The June issue included the following notice:

pressed brick and stone front, and cost $10,000.

Architect C. S. Corwin : For George Blossom and Warren McArthur, two two-story and attic residences, of pressed brick and frame ; to be erected on Forty-ninth street and Kenwood avenue ; they will have all the improvements, and cost $16,000.

The initials "C.S." stand for none other than Cecil Sherman Corwin, Frank Lloyd Wright's good friend and confidant, who must have been willing to help Wright with his "*la tromperie*." It is likely that neither Dankmar Adler nor Louis Sullivan would have been curious enough about the work of an independent architect to concern themselves with any more of the details about these two houses other than what they might have read in this issue of the local trade journal.

Over the years, this house, along with all the other bootleg commissions, has been confirmed to have been designed by Frank Lloyd Wright. The most common reason cited for Wright's moonlighting career was his need for more revenue, not only for daily household expenses but for his lavish lifestyle, too. However, these commissions also gave Wright the opportunity to study various architectural styles and explore his own ideas without any supervision from Sullivan.

Researchers have proposed that Wright's inspiration for the Blossom house was the H.A.C. Taylor house in Newport, Rhode Island, designed by McKim, Mead & White. The plans for the Taylor house were drawn up in 1882, but the home was not actually built until 1885. The first published drawings of the completed home began appearing in trade journals in 1887. The New York offices of Henry C. Meyer were publishing a weekly journal called *The Sanitary Engineer and Construction Record*. In the May 4, 1887 issue, a drawing of the Taylor House was published. Wright had arrived in Chicago in 1886 and was working for Joseph Lyman Silsbee by this time. Silsbee may have subscribed to this publication; there is a drawing for the Silsbee & Marling house in Buffalo, New York, on the page preceding the drawing for the Taylor house. There were also notices of other works by Silsbee & Marling in the March 1887 issue. The April 1887 issue of this same journal mentions the Edgewater, Illinois subdivision that Silsbee was designing for J.L. Cochrane. So, the question remains: Would Wright have seen a drawing of the Taylor house and been so impressed by it that he would retain this thought and design a similar house five years later? To borrow a line from a TV courtroom drama: "Yes, it could be possible."

Wright would have been aware of the Colonial Revival–style design that McKim, Mead & White used for the Taylor house. He

Top: Undated portrait of Dankmar Adler, Chicago, Illinois. D.R. Clarke, photographer. *Richard Nickel Archive, Ryerson and Burnham Art and Architecture Archives, Art Institute of Chicago. Digital file #201006_110711-022.*

Bottom: Portrait of Louis H. Sullivan, Chicago, Illinois, circa 1900. *Sullivaniana Collection, Ryerson and Burnham Art and Architecture Archives, Art Institute of Chicago. Digital file #193101. LHS_Portrait_1900.*

Opposite, inset: Chicago History Museum, ICHi-182715.

could have found and reviewed pictures and drawings of this style, also. Since Wright did not leave us any documentation as to what might have inspired him, it is challenging to say one building out of all the examples he could have found was the primary source for his inspiration. And, since Wright was designing this house clandestinely, he would not have engaged in any discussions of the pros and cons of Colonial Revival architecture with his office mates and certainly not with Louis Sullivan. He would not have shared his design ideas for this home, either. The design Wright created for the Blossom house was quite different from what he would be doing in the future. He would soon come to abhor these revival styles, along with other architectural styles derived from European examples.

The thought of Frank Lloyd Wright designing the perfect example of a Colonial Revival home may seem very foreign to someone who only knows of his later work, but the fact remains he did. His work on this house shows that if designing buildings for traditional clients in the styles that were common in the United States was all that Frank Lloyd Wright was inclined to do, he would have had a good career doing just that. Of the twenty or so elements found on the exterior of homes designed in the Colonial Revival vernacular, Wright used several on the Blossom house.

The house is a five-thousand-square-foot symmetrical building. It is a large rectangle, with two semicircular features installed on the front and rear facades to give the building balance. The front porch and the conservatory to the rear of the house make up these two harmonizing elements.

The front elevation shows the foundation is brick-based; this feature strongly attaches the house to the ground. Wright came to believe that a building and its site should complement each other, and this foundation of earth-toned Roman bricks allowed him to achieve that. The roof of the front porch is supported by Ionic columns that rise from the porch floor to the eaves of the classically styled roof. The home is two stories high, and the main roof has eaves that extend from the exterior walls to create a sheltering cover to the top of the house. Another component of the Colonial Revival style that Wright uses is Palladian windows on the first floor. These windows have a dominant lintel and are made up of three parts, including a large central pane of plain glass, two side windows and an arched glass panel above the central window. These windows allow an ample amount of light into each of the first-floor rooms.

The house has wood clapboard siding covering the entire building. The main entry door is located on the porch. On entering, one finds a comfortable entrance hall with the library situated to the left and the amply sized reception room to the right. These rooms, along with the dining room, have rounded arched doorways that are trimmed in wood on the wall edges. From the front door and through the hall, one can see the inglenook across the living room. This focal point, along with the view from the library into the dining room and into the conservatory, forces us to see the house the way Wright intended us to see it. The living room includes an outdoor terrace; this space, along with the conservatory, are examples of ways Wright created environments that allow people to be close to nature and effortlessly join the outdoors with the indoor spaces.

In the living room, Wright included a distinctive hearth with wood trim that is set back into the wall; there are two bench seats on either side of the fireplace. Wright uses a ceramic tile on the facing wall of the fireplace and then extends this same tile onto the floor; the tile stops at the edge of the inglenook where the wood slat floor of the living room begins.

The first floor has a tall wooden baseboard with four wide panels of wood above that. Wright provided the Blossoms with pieces of built-in furniture throughout the house, particularly in the conservatory: the built-in seating covers the steam heat radiators that are spaced along the curved outer wall. The second floor has five bedrooms or, as Wright labeled them, "chambers." There is a large full bathroom on the second floor. On the original plans, two of the bedrooms were shown to have wash sinks included. In each chamber room, Wright included either a closet or a dressing room. The main hall includes more closets, as well. The stairwell is multilevel and includes a skylight. The banister of the stairway creates a waterfall pattern.

The art glass throughout the house is beautiful. In Doreen Ehrlich's book *Frank Lloyd Wright Glass*, she calls the art glass forms that surround the main entryway "curvilinear, intersecting forms." The art glass windows in the stair landing are a beautiful combination of wreaths and ribbons. Art glass and molded forms such as wreaths, garlands, and flowing banners were all common elements of decoration in Colonial Revival architecture.

When a style is being "revived," designers will not try to replicate the original designs exactly; more often, they will bring back certain elements to allow the home's occupants to reimagine the original style in the new work they are producing. From the late 1800s and through the 1940s, when architects were designing in the Colonial Revival style, they were really modeling Georgian architecture, which was transplanted to the American colonies in the 1700s. To make this revived style new (or look new), elements from the Federal style and Georgian designs were often combined with existing Colonial styles.

Wright said of the Blossom house that he did not have the time to supervise the construction as he was busy at Adler & Sullivan's office. For him to travel by train from his downtown office to Kenwood and then on to the construction site and back would be more than an hour round trip, and any discussions with the contractor would have used up even more time than Wright could have spared.

In 1907, with the advent of the automobile, George Blossom commissioned Wright to add a garage to his homesite. Wright was happy to oblige him, and he provided Blossom with two options: one design would accommodate a horse-drawn carriage, and the second design would house a motorcar. George selected the second design. The building was two stories and held an apartment for the Blossoms' chauffeur in the second-floor space.

In the 1900s, wealthy Chicago residents began moving from their southside homes to the north shore communities of Rogers Park, Winnetka, Highland Park, and other small towns that were being settled north of the city. Sheridan Road, Milwaukee Avenue and Green Bay Avenue gave these new suburbanites easy access to the city of Chicago, but there were also options for commuter trains and interurban train service into the city. In 1915, the Blossoms sold their home and moved to an exclusive section of Winnetka in a neighborhood called Hubbard Woods. They did not seek out Frank Lloyd Wright for their new home. In 1930, with their children off and married, George and Carrie had moved to the resident suites of the Drake Tower Hotel on Lake Shore Drive in Chicago. In the 1930s, the Blossoms began to spend time in Pasadena, California. While on a trip back to Chicago in June 1938, Carrie became ill; her health did not improve, and she passed away on June 26, 1938. After the family's funeral services ended, Carrie was interred at Rose Hill Cemetery in Chicago. In 1940, George listed his home address in Pasadena, California. In 1942, at the age of eighty-eight, George joined Carrie in eternal rest while in Pasadena. His family returned him to Chicago, and he was buried next to his wife.

The Blossom house is a stately home with a design that would hold up in any fashionable neighborhood—or it could be set high on a bluff along a river's edge and still look beautiful. The design shows Wright's ability to work with a classical style of architecture to create an aesthetically pleasing house that is comfortable and allows the residents to enjoy both the home's inside and outdoor spaces. We also see Wright's penchant for blending the inside of a home with nature.

The Blossom house meets the criteria established to determine its status as a bootleg house. The construction of the home took place in 1892, which is well within Wright's bootleg phase. George Blossom was, in fact, the client, and he had a personal relationship with Wright: he sought out Wright as his architect. The plans include quite a bit of detail, so it is very unlikely Wright would have worked on them at his desk just outside of Sullivan's office. Wright did try to conceal his involvement in this commission; as noted earlier, the original announcement for this commission attributed the design to Cecil Corwin. Since this home meets all the criteria for a bootleg commission, it should be classified as Wright's first bootleg house.

One lot to the east of the Blossoms' home was the home of Warren McArthur. This commission's identification number is 9205, and it is the next building we will review because of its proximity to the Blossoms' house.

The Emmond home, which is in La Grange, Illinois, has inventory number 9202. The recorded number for the Thomas Gale house in Oak Park, Illinois, is 9203. The discussion of these homes will take place with the other homes in those respective villages.

The Dr. Allison Harlan house is numbered 9204, and the discussion of that home will follow that of the McArthur home.

Ironically, the story of the Warren McArthur house has its beginnings in Dubuque, Iowa, just as the Blossoms' family story did.

Warren McArthur Home

Kenwood, Illinois, 1892

Warren McArthur was born in 1856. His parents, Charles and Martha, were living in Dubuque, Iowa, at that time. Minnie Weston, who would become Warren's wife, was the daughter of Reuel and Olive Weston. She was born in 1860, in Xenia, Ohio, which is about sixteen miles east of the city of Dayton. Xenia was a railroad town, and Minnie's father was a railroad engineer. Warren's father became a railroad man, too, but his forte was numbers, and he became an accountant for the Chicago, Clinton, Dubuque, and Minnesota (CCD&M) Railroad. By the late 1870s, Charles had become the paymaster for the railroad.

Reuel was also employed by the CCD&M Railroad as a train engineer, and in time, he moved his family to Dubuque, Iowa.

As Warren and Minnie grew up in the same town, they may have had mutual friends or even gone to school together, but exactly how they met is not known. In 1880, twenty-four-year-old Warren married his twenty-year-

Warren McArthur house. *Courtesy of Douglas M. Steiner, Edmonds, WA.*

old sweetheart, Minnie. Warren began his working career as a clerk for the firm of Raymond Brothers & Hill, which ran a store selling crockery and glassware in Dubuque.

The city of Dubuque was founded on the banks of the Mississippi River and was named after Julien Dubuque, who was one of the original settlers in this area. Since the town's inception, moving freight has always been an important part of the city's history, whether it was on the barges that plied the Mississippi or on boxcars being shuttled through the city's freight yards. The people who work in these shipping industries do not work nine-to-five schedules. When the boats or trains are ready, the people who work on them must be ready to go, too, no matter what the hour. One tool that workers for both industries would have with them from late afternoon to early morning would have been lanterns. Train line signal men would have been using lanterns all day long. The railways and riverboat shipping companies would have been buying lanterns by the case load from the 1850s through the mid-1900s. Warren McArthur must have seen the need for lantern salespeople, because in 1878, he left his position at Raymond Brothers & Hill and went to work for a company called Dennis & Wheeler. This company sold a brand of lanterns called the Irwin Lantern. In 1881, when Warren had a steady job at a good company, the McArthurs had their first child, a boy they named Albert. After a couple of different company mergers, Warren found himself working for the R.E. Dietz Company as a traveling lantern salesperson. Then, in 1882, he became the co-manager of the company's Chicago sales office, along with John E. Dietz. The McArthur family had moved to one of the fastest-growing cities in the United States: Chicago, Illinois. And they did their part to help the city grow by having three more children of their own. Warren Jr. was born in 1885; another son, Charles, was born in 1890; and finally, a daughter, Louise, entered the world in 1895. In 1897, the Dietz company bought the Steam Gauge Lantern Company and relocated its Chicago office from its Lake Street address to a new office on Randolph Street. McArthur and Dietz were still managing this new office.

Whether it was through business dealings or at All Souls Church, the MacArthurs and the Blossoms became close friends even before they became neighbors. Warren also befriended another young man, a draftsman named Frank Lloyd Wright. In 1892, the McArthurs had outgrown their home on Fifty-First Street in Chicago, which was just west of Washington Park, and they were looking to move to a neighborhood more befitting the social standing of a well-paid sales manager for a successful company. They chose the lot right next door to their family friend George Blossom on Kenwood Avenue. The neighborhood was the logical choice for the McArthurs, as Warren was already a member of the fashionable Kenwood Social Club. The purpose of the club was to provide social activities for both male and female members who were willing and able to pay the one-hundred-dollar registration fee along with forty dollars in annual dues. The McArthurs also followed the Blossoms' lead in their choice of an architect: their other family friend Frank Lloyd Wright.

There is no surviving correspondence between the McArthurs and Wright, so we do not know who made the choice of the Dutch Colonial style for the home. As noted earlier, the first notice of the McArthurs' home was in the June 1892 issue of *Inland Architect*. And the architect for the McArthur house, like the Blossoms', was listed as Cecil Corwin! However, we now know that this home is another of those designed by Wright, in his home studio in Oak Park.

Researchers have questioned why Wright did not design the McArthurs' home in a style that may have been more complementary to the Blossoms' house, rather than a style that was completely different. As it was, in this case, the owners were friendly toward each other, and both had an address on Kenwood Avenue. Was the choice for this style of home Wright's, or was it the clients'? The surname McArthur is from Gaelic traditions, and Minnie's family name was Weston, which was a common Anglo-Saxon name. It was not likely that they were trying to have their home linked back to a historical family farm.

Wright was experimenting with distinctive styles when he designed the Blossom and McArthur houses. As noted earlier, many writers have made mention of the idea that Wright's inspiration for the Blossom house was the Taylor house, but this is just an assumption; there is no verifiable proof for this assertion. However, these same critics have not found a suitable Dutch Colonial building to compare Wright's McArthur house to.

Wright was not trying, at that time, to build his reputation on designing multiple buildings in the Colonial Revival style or the Dutch Colonial design. He was not trying to establish himself as the designer of a whole subdivision with houses built using a similar thematic design—although Wright would venture forth with an idea for land planning in 1932 with the development called Broadacre City. There would be no practical reason for Wright to design complementary houses next to each other, other than for convenience sake. However, we will see this happen in Oak Park as Wright is finishing out his bootleg phase.

Instead of asking why Wright did not do something, we should focus on what he did do.

The Dutch Colonial–style home is an enigma. The style may evoke a certain building design in one's mind, but this style of home was not brought to the North American continent by Dutch settlers.

The early Dutch settlers built their homes out of available materials; they were usually one-room buildings, which may have had a loft for storage. The Dutch Colonial house that architects were beginning to design in the 1880s suggested the idea of a loving family home on the farm. The Dutch Colonial Revival homes that had become popular in the late 1880s could include atypical features as long as a few basic design elements were used. The gambrel roof, or barn roof, was essential; it is the one feature that clearly defines this style of home. This style of roof has two matching sides; the roof is wide and has a slight slope at the top and then drops off sharply, until it flares back out to create broad eaves. Since the house is beholden to the roof's construction, the interior of the building is simply planned. The support of the roof is from trusses that span the space and have columns on each end. There is no interior post to support the roof; therefore, the space below is completely open. These homes typically had stud walls with a covering of wood panels installed vertically on the interior and had clapboard siding on

Dutch Colonial–style home. Saturday Evening Post, *May 22, 1920.*

the exterior. However, there are examples of Dutch Colonial homes with stone or brick facades, too. The open space below the roof is adapted to create living quarters. Dormers on the roof are also quite common. Other features found in a Dutch Colonial home would include Dutch doors, which are panel doors that have two halves, so the top half can be open to allow light and air into the house, while the lower half can be closed, keeping animals out and the children in. Typically, the fireplace(s) would be at the end of the house, and windows would flank the chimney. The home would have a front porch and main entry door included on one of the longer sides of the building. The windows would be placed symmetrically with the first- and second-floor windows paired vertically. The first floor of the Dutch Colonial home would be one room deep and two to three rooms wide. Since the fireplaces were in fixed locations at the ends of the house, you would not find the other rooms pinwheeled around the fireplace, like in an American four-square home.

The home Wright designed for the McArthur family is a Dutch Colonial due to its gambrel roof, its dormers and the main entry located on the side of the house, but other features found in this style of house are missing. The McArthur house is perpendicular to the street; there is a porch to the street side that is on a concrete foundation, but it does not include the main entry. The base wall of the home is Roman brick and rises from the ground to the first-floor windowsills. The exterior wall space between the sill line and the eaves is plaster, as are the gambrel walls of the second and third floors. The upper portion of the front facade has two large double-hung windows for each bedroom and a large, arched, framed window installed on the third floor.

The main entry door is on the left side of the house, and the door itself seems to be set low. Wright used a system of contraction and expansion in his buildings throughout his career. As you step through the door, you must, depending on your height, crouch slightly to enter. Once inside, you stand upright, and the room expands with you. Wright creates the feeling of expansion by placing the vestibule three steps below the main floor. There is a parapet wall that includes spindles, which increases the height of this small space. As you are standing in the vestibule, Wright forces you to look up to find your way out of this space. The low wall section ends with a newel post that includes a lovely little stained-glass lamp. As you enter the hall, the parlor is to your right and a fireplace is to the left; across the space are the stairs to the second floor. To the right and beyond the parlor is the living room, which includes a second fireplace, and there are access doors from both the parlor and living room to what was originally an open terrace. Throughout Wright's career, he continually spoke of breaking the box—he did not want his buildings to be just boxes next to boxes—so here in the McArthur house, he includes three large bay windows, one in each of the major rooms on the first floor. The windows have leaded, diamond-shaped glass panes. This design allows ample light into the room and grants the homeowner the ability to see out. The art glass acts as a screen from onlookers on the sidewalk. The cantilevered bay windows sit slightly beyond the wall; the windows are supported by diamond-shaped brick corbels.

The prospect of designing a home for a friend such as Warren allowed Wright to create unique art glass for the McArthur dining room. From the entry hall, there are two doorways that lead into the dining room. Each door has a wood frame with glass panels. These panels are as tall as the full height of the doors. Wright did not provide us with his inspiration for the geometric art glass design: Could it be a stylized grass plant or corn stalk, or is it based on another natural form? Doreen Ehrlich refers to this design as having an arrow motif. Regardless of the origin, the panels are a wonderful combination of clear and colored glass, and the cabinets in the built-in buffet have the same pattern used for the glass door cabinets.

The second floor holds six bedrooms and a large bathroom, while the third floor is one large great room with a barrel-vaulted ceiling. Wright would use this feature of a barrel-vaulted ceiling in his own house in 1895, for the second-floor playroom. There is another bedroom on the third floor that is plain but functional. This might have been a room for someone who worked in the house. The third-floor great room holds an arched art glass window that forms maybe a stylized seed pod or butterfly wings—one really cannot be sure. The date of the McArthur home clearly falls within Wright's bootleg phase, as documented by the notice in the June 1882 issue of the *Inland Architect*. Warren McArthur and Wright were close friends, so Warren likely sought out Frank to design this home. For Wright's clandestine work, he pulled his friend Cecil Corwin into the scheme to sign off on building permits and to generate the advertisement in the *Inland Architect*. Wright would have completed the plans in his home studio rather than his office at Adler & Sullivan.

In Wright's work on the McArthur house, he shows us he can set aside the plan for the Blossom house and produce something completely different but still in a classical style. We also see Wright pulling in his own ideas, which will be staples of his Prairie period: the concrete water table, the Roman brick courses anchoring the house to the ground, and the sheltering roof that protects the house. We will see some of these same features employed on Wright's next bootleg home.

The McArthur house also meets all the criteria to establish it as a bootleg commission, in the same order as the Blossom house. Therefore, this commission will be considered another of Wright's bootleg houses.

The year 1892 would see Wright take on more commissions without the firm's knowledge, but he also worked on two assignments that were projects of the firm.

The commissions that are numbered 9207 and 9208 are reserved for two buildings Wright worked on during his tenure at Adler & Sullivan. There are no drawings for either of the projects in Wright's archives, but comments made by Wright suggest he had done a considerable amount of independent work in designing these buildings. The first building became known as the Albert Sullivan House.

Albert was Louis's younger brother; however, he was not the one for whom the home was originally built. Louis was the first resident in the home. Project number 9208 is the inventory number of the Victoria Hotel, which was built in Chicago Heights, Illinois. The hotel project was for Victor Faulkner. Wright had a free hand in the hotel complex designing. It was also the project he was working on when he had the break with Sullivan. Neither of these two commissions can be considered bootleg designs. Wright collaborated closely with Louis Sullivan on the designs of the Albert Sullivan house, and a second architect from Adler & Sullivan's firm named Louis Claude also worked on the Victoria Hotel commission.

While Wright used two classical styles of architecture for his two Kenwood homes, he tried something altogether different for the home in North Kenwood. Dr. Harlan's house finds its place in the chronological order of Wright's work at number 9204.

Dr. Allison W. Harlan Home

North Kenwood, Illinois, 1892
Demolished 1963

To his friends in the field of dentistry, Allison Harlan, DDS, was a man for the ages; to others, he became what people might describe as a scoundrel for leaving his wife and their six children. Among Dr. Harlan's professional triumphs, he also had another unique claim to fame. Harlan may have been the first person to suggest that the city of Chicago should host the World's Columbian Exhibition. He made this suggestion when he wrote an open letter to the residents of Chicago, which was published in the *Chicago Times* on February 6, 1882, proposing Chicago as the host city for the upcoming World's Columbian Exhibition. The exhibition was to be a celebration to commemorate Christopher Columbus's first voyage to the Americas in 1492.

There was little reaction to Harlan's suggestion, and when the leadership committees were established to promote the idea of having the fair in Chicago, Harlan's name was not seen on any of the membership lists; however, you did see the likes of George Pullman of the Pullman Motor Car Company; Potter Palmer, the real estate tycoon and owner of the Palmer House Hotel; and Daniel Burnham, one of the principals of the architectural firm Burnham & Root. When Chicago officials were notified that their bid to host the Columbian Exhibition had been approved, Daniel Burnham was appointed to be the managing architect for all the fair's buildings, grounds, and support facilities.

According to Harlan's obituary, which appeared in the 1909 *Annual Dental Digest*, he was born in Indianapolis, Indiana, in 1851, As a young man, he went to work in the dental office of Drs. Kilgore & Helm. He stayed there until 1869, when he left and moved to Chicago, where he opened his own dental office. Harlan's obituary also noted that he had been active in dental societies throughout the United States, and he was

Dr. Allison Harlan house. *Courtesy of Douglas M. Steiner, Edmonds, WA.*

the driving force behind the creation of the trade journal *The Dental Review*, for which he was the first editor.

Wright's design of the Harlan house became a defining moment in his career, and it is a design he was so fond of that he had a photograph of this early home included in an article from the June 1900 issue of the journal *Architectural Review*. The article was written by Robert C. Spencer Jr. and titled "The Work of Frank Lloyd Wright, from 1893 to 1900." The article was intended to be both a written essay and a pictorial review of Wright's work after his independent career began. However, two photographs are of designs completed prior to 1893. These images are of the Cooper house plan, from 1890, and the Harlan house, from 1892. The inclusion of these images attests to Wright's fondness for these projects. The Harlan house was also included in an exhibition held in Florence, Italy, in 1951, titled *Sixty Years of Living Architecture.*

Oscar Stonorov, a Philadelphia-based architect, was the curator for the show in Florence. Stonorov did not want to include the Harlan house photos in the retrospective of Wright's work. However, Wright stipulated that they must be included. This show included over nine hundred exhibits, including drawings, models, and photographs. Stonorov completed an initial schedule of the items he wished to have displayed—which was a list that Wright did not agree with at all. He prepared his own catalog of items for the show. In Wright's plan, the projects to be displayed from the year 1893 were to include four works from the firm of Adler & Sullivan that Wright had worked on and the Harlan house. The Harlan residence was the only building Wright chose to have displayed that was from his moonlighting period. In 1956, Wright told Harlan's daughter that the Harlan house was the "first house built my own way." For as much as Wright may have had a fondness for the Harlan house design, he was not too willing to let the world know about his involvement in it. The public announcement for the home came in the *Inland Architect* of July 1891 with the following caption:

Architect C. S. Corwin: For Dr. A. W. Harlan, a two-story residence of pressed brick, stone and frame; to have hardwood interior, steam heat, and cost $15,000; it will be built on Greenwood avenue and Forty-fourth place.

Chicago History Museum, ICHi-182714.

Wright again asked Cecil Corwin to be listed as the architect for another project. Corwin was now sharing office space with his fellow architect George W. Maher in Chicago at 28 La Salle Street; he would do so from 1890 to 1893.

Even though Wright would later complain to Louis Sullivan that he felt he had not broken the terms of his contract, the fact that he was having Corwin run advertisements contradicts that statement.

The house that Wright designed was quite different from the shingle-style Queen Anne homes he used for other bootleg designs; Wright was clearly experimenting. Having just finished the Charnley home on Astor Street in Chicago, which was done under Sullivan's supervision, Wright was free to let his own ideas flow from his creative mind. One of the ideas that drew Sullivan and Wright together was their love of nature and the belief that natural forms should be used as the basis for a building's ornamentation. Wright first experienced Sullivan's theories in the designs of the Auditorium Building. Sullivan wanted to use ornamentation that was sympathetic to nature, and Wright would later speak of his architecture as organic, meaning that the landscaping, the building, the furniture, and adornments such as art glass were designed to create a unified whole. Wright's first example of this edict, which would become a guiding principle of his architecture, was the design of the Harlan house. Features that would become commonplace in Wright's Prairie homes can be found in the Harlan house, too. If we could stand in front of the house today, we would see a unique building.

The central entryway is gone, replaced by a long cloister, a path to the left of the house where the main door was securely screened from the street. The veranda with a baluster railing, as we saw on the MacHarg house, is now a protected porch, with a solid wall shielding the residents; the lower portion of the front facade includes large casement windows, not the typical double-hung windows others were using.

Instead of a steeply peaked roof, as seen on the shingle-style homes, Wright used a hip roof that included four planes, which extended down from a central ridge. The roof is broken by dormers, which add light and cool breezes into the second-floor bedrooms. The second floor has two balconies, one that faces the front elevation to the east and a second one that faces north. Both balconies have decorative wood panels hand cut by a skilled craftsman in a pattern reminiscent of the panels seen on the Charnley house's interior stairwell. These panels created privacy for anyone who was sitting on the balcony and enjoying the out-of-doors. The underside of the balconies is decorated with another set of panels. These panels have an oak leaf motif carved into each corner and a geometric design cut into the field of the panel. The balconies have support rods connecting the base of the structure to the underside of the eaves. At the roofline, the supports are connected to each other by what might be wrought iron or wood cut braces. These were designed with a naturalistic pattern suggestive of a leafy vine growing between the supports.

In Wright's original design, the interior of the first floor was to be wide open. When passing over the threshold, you would have entered a large reception hall, where to your left would have been the staircase to the second floor, with a newel post that had a Sullivanesque-style floral relief carved into it and a sconce candleholder for lighting. On ascending to the second floor, there were six bedrooms, with access to the balconies, and toilet facilities. The staircase created an open well that was two stories high and surrounded by a railing with upright supports. This open space would provide ventilation for the home during the hot Chicago summers. Returning to the home's entry, situated to the right would have been a large living room that stretched across the front of the house. Across the hall would be the library, which would be a quiet place for reading; this room was expanded using a bay window. The original plan called for a double-sided fireplace set into the wall separating the main hall and the library; this location created a focal point to carry your eyes across the room. Since this home was designed so early in Wright's career, he had not yet developed the force of personality that would allow him to rebuff the wishes of his clients. Wright would acquire the ability to contradict his clients' ideas while at the same time beguiling them with a justification of how *his* plan would make their experience of living in one of *his* homes much more rewarding. However, Harlan insisted that the spacious living room be divided into two parlors. Wright was able to temper Harlan's idea by installing only a partition wall in the living room, which divided the room in half but maintained the view from the entryway that Wright had intended. Harlan also wanted the fireplace relocated to the north wall of the now-divided living room. Wright made this change, too, but he was probably not happy about it.

Just past the second-floor staircase would have been the breakfast nook, facing south to take advantage of the morning sun. The main dining room would have been located on the opposite side of the house. Both the dining room and the breakfast area would have had individual doorways to and from the kitchen.

Wright would always design the bedroom spaces in his homes as personal spaces. Conversely, he also kept redefining the common spaces on the first floor to be open, and he allowed the rooms to flow together.

The Harlan house should be included on the roster of bootleg designs. It is not formally known how Harlan and Wright came to meet, but the other criteria listed have been met. Harlan was in fact Wright's client, not Cecil Corwin's. This home is not included in the inventory of homes designed by the firm of Adler & Sullivan. The construction plans for this house no longer exist, but there is a photograph of the Harlan house in the Frank Lloyd Wright archives that is identified as commission number 9204. The Harlan house is another of Wright's bootleg commissions.

As the 1880s were winding down, things were not going well for Harlan; he had become an officer of the Globe Bank in Chicago, and due to creative accounting with the bank's deposits by its president, Charles W. Spaulding, the bank was found to be in arrears in 1887. As the actions of the bank's staff were investigated, the fear of indictments hung over Harlan's head from 1887 to 1889. Spaulding was eventually found guilty of embezzlement. There was some speculation that Harlan would be sent up for trial as well, but the story fell out of the headlines after 1899 with no mention of Harlan ever being prosecuted. Harlan was able to stay out of the papers for the next few years, until 1902, when an article was published in the June 6 edition of the *Chicago Tribune* reporting that Harlan's wife was suing him for divorce; she cited him for drunkenness, cruelty, and desertion. But according to the doctor's obituary, it seems 1902 ended better than it began. Yes, the Harlans were divorced, but shortly after his divorce, Harlan remarried Eliza (Mary) Murison; they then moved to New York State, where Harlan continued in the practice of dentistry and he and his second wife lived out their days. Harlan passed away in 1909; he was buried in the Kensico Cemetery, located in Valhalla, New York. His second wife, Mary, followed him in 1929. Harlan's first wife, Aliza, did not remarry, as she was left to raise the couple's six children. She died in 1918 and was buried in Forest Lawn Cemetery in Forest Park, Illinois, a suburb just outside the city limits of Chicago.

The story of the Harlan house must also include an account of its unfortunate demise, as the home was demolished after a fire in 1963. Harlan had kept ownership of the house until 1903 or 1904. Beginning in 1904, the Chicago address books listed John P. Byrne living at the Greenwood Avenue home. The ownership records of the Harlan house are scarce, but prior to 1920, the Byrne family either sold or vacated the building. The building was then left vacant for many years and eventually became a local haunt for the neighborhood. To bring the building back from its dilapidated state, a small nursing home was established there, but by 1963, the building had been abandoned again. Later in 1963, the building was set ablaze by an unknown arsonist, and the damage was so extensive that the remaining structure had to be torn down. After the fire, a man named Richard Nichel, who was an architectural historian and photographer, documented the building's condition. His photographs show the detail of the underside panels of the balcony, which clearly show an oak leaf pattern Wright had designed seventy years before.

When Wright was designing the Harlan house, he did not use any of the features of the Queen Anne or shingle-style designs, nor did he use any of the characteristics of the classical styles he had used in the Blossom or McArthur homes. It was only at Harlan's insistence that the living room was divided into two parlors, but even then, instead of using a full-height wall to create separate rooms, Wright was able to keep some of the openness using a parapet wall. The two second-floor balconies and front porch were the outdoor areas Wright included for his clients. The location of the main entry door placed to the side down a covered walkway—and the other features listed above—were Wright's own ideas for changing the way American houses would be seen and used in the future.

Wright's bootleg phase included work in two Chicago suburbs, La Grange and Oak Park. Another home to be considered a bootleg design was in the village of La Grange. The lands around what would eventually be called La Grange was settled in the 1830s, and the village was incorporated in 1879.

La Grange was incorporated after the population had expanded with new residents moving from Chicago after the Great Chicago Fire of 1871. The first project associated with Frank Lloyd Wright was completed in 1890; however, it was more of an exercise in design than a set of drawings for a client looking for a new home. The first of Wright's designs that was purported to be in the western suburb of La Grange, Illinois, was the Henry Cooper project, numbered 9004. The project shows how some facts may just be jiggled a little bit so that, if we are not careful, we might find ourselves coming to conclusions that do not hold up to the bright light of truth. After a review of the Cooper project, we will discuss two commissions that were built in La Grange.

THE LA GRANGE HOMES

Henry Cooper Project

La Grange, Illinois, 1890
Unbuilt

The Henry Cooper house project was the first unbuilt commission that has been suggested to have been a bootleg project. In the Frank Lloyd Wright archives, the plans for this project are numbered 9004. These drawings are dated to the year 1890. The plan sheet that is numbered 9004.002 clearly states in the lower left-hand corner that the drawing is a "plan of the Cooper house arranged to be built on a corner lot in La Grange Illinois."

There are three plan sheets for this project; each of the three drawings is two dimensional, and the main homesite is seen from a bird's-eye view. The project was never forwarded to completion, and one wonders if the Coopers were even clients of Wright. There seems to be some anecdotal evidence that Henry Cooper, who was a real estate attorney, met Frank Lloyd Wright to discuss a house plan prior to 1890, but for whatever reason, this discussion never went any further.

However, in a book titled *La Grange Park and La Grange Illinois* published in 1999, there is a photograph of the Cooper family home from 1887. This building is a large, three-story home with a brick foundation. It has a large porch with a railing. The home has a large gable roof with one small dormer facing the front of the home. The photograph is grainy, but the home looks to be clad in shingles. The first floor has a bay window to the left of the front porch, and a second set of first-floor windows is to the back of the house; there does look to be another set of windows to the right of the porch, as an outline of a window frame can be seen, but the remainder of the space is obscured by a small tree. All the windows are double hung, except for the dormer window, which may have been an awning window. The front gable has an architectural feature of four balusters perched on a shelf that is held up by brackets and is covering another window. There are also neatly trimmed walkways heading up to the house from two directions. The photograph even shows the family's chicken coop to the rear of the home. The house has elements of the Queen Anne style, but it does not resemble the plan Wright created in 1890. This completed house is not included in the Wright archives. It seems very unlikely that Cooper would have been searching for an architect to design him a home in 1890, after having just built this home in 1887. It is, however, possible that just like Wright's design for the Unitarian chapel in Sioux City, this sketch was an effort in design and not a bona fide commission.

The numbering system used for the drawings for this house may have only been used for cataloging purposes, as drawing number 9004.003 is an unmeasured sketch with little detail. Drawing number 9004.001 shows a more formal house with identifiable walls, room assignments, and landscaping.

The drawing number 9004.002 shows the completed house and a barn that has been placed on the drawing and is seen from the front elevation and not the bird's-eye view. This barn building is surprisingly like the building design in Wright's drawing numbered 8701. This was the drawing that Wright said he had created in Madison and that he showed to Sullivan during his first job interview. From the view Wright creates of the barn, you can see the arched entrance for horse-drawn buggies; there is a long wall to the right of this entry. The wall is detailed with what was intended to be a wooden belt line feature that projects from the wall and travels to both ends of the structure. The barn has a shingled hip roof with eaves that extend out past the wall, in the same manner as Wright's Prairie-style houses would be designed. The main barn is one story, but there is a two-story extension toward the front left side of the building. The entrance to the barn is covered by a separate turret; the room above the entrance looks to have a stone base and slat-covered windows. There is also a wide chimney toward the rear of the building. The drawing of the barn has some of the same features that are included in the presentation drawing Wright used in his interview with Sullivan. The 1887 drawing has a roofline that is similar; however, the two-story element is placed to the right of center; in 1890, Wright moved that feature to the left of center. The belt line feature is not included in the 1887 drawing, and this older drawing includes some windows that are not present in the later version.

Returning to the plans for the house, we can see from the bird's-eye perspective that the roofline is shown as a continuous, lightly dotted line that follows the perimeter of the house and shows where the peaks and faces of the hip roof would have been. From our vantage point perched above the house, we can see where each of the first-floor rooms will be and where the stairways and exterior walls will be located, but what we do not readily see are interior walls. There are abutments at strategic locations to create supports for the eventual ceiling and roof, and there are partition walls to separate the music room from the library in the family's home. These openings do not include doors; therefore, the plan allows for an easy transition from one room to another. On closer inspection, we can see that there will be doors installed to cordon off the kitchen and keep the powder room private, respectively.

To access the main entry of the home, a visitor must walk up the steps to a broad sidewalk. There is a formal garden in front of the house, and as one approaches, they must choose which of the two bilateral walks they will take to make their final approach to the front door. After the final few steps are climbed, and on reaching the front door, the more observant visitor may have noticed that nine steps have been transverse and at least four turns were made to achieve this destination. In time, the path to the main entry of Wright's homes would become part of the allure of his designs: the sheltered entrance to be arrived at by way of a pathway of discovery. On entering the home, a large hall is the first room to be encountered. The room is a cube that has three wings projecting from it in a symmetrical form. From our vantage point, we do not see any furniture; in time, Wright would be designing both built-in and freestanding furniture for his homes. He would also design complementary light fixtures, carpets, and art glass windows for the exterior walls and even for partitions within the house.

From the main entry hall, we scan the area to determine the extent of the house. To our right is the passageway to the family's bedroom wing; toward the rear of the house is a porte cochere. To our left and somewhat behind us is the music room, which has a bay window. There is no grand piano yet, but the room seems to have been sized for one. From the music room we can pass into the library, where there are added details for the placement of bookshelves, but no writing desk or chairs are seen just yet. Finally, we can step down into the pavilion, the smallest room on the tour so far; it is well lit with large windows to the north and west, and there is a secondary exit to the front walk, if needed. Walking through the small vestibule, one can enter the dining room. The room is circular, and there are multiple windows and alcoves where built-in storage units could be placed. To the left is a short hall that leads to the amply sized kitchen and pantry. The exit to the barn is also in this direction. This overhead view and this visual tour are all Wright provides. After all, this is only a plan; no schematics need to be drawn yet. But we cannot help wondering what the exterior will look like. Will it complement the proposed barn? It is likely that it will. Will the exterior be sided with shingles or clapboard siding, or will Wright be creating something new? We are left to only speculate. In fact, "speculate" is a well-chosen word here because this project never did leave the drawing board.

One of the curious aspects of this plan is the resemblance of Wright's plan to the plans for two homes that were designed by the firm of McKim, Mead & White, whose offices were in New York City. This firm had several commissions on the East Coast in the late 1800s and early 1900s. In Samuel G. White's book, *The Houses of McKim, Mead and White*, he writes:

> *During the period between 1879 and 1921, McKim, Mead & White became the largest and most important architecture office in America, if not in the world. With a staff that grew to over one hundred, the firm became the model for the modern architectural practice.*

With this type of reputation, surely Wright would have known of their work.

Of the two homes in question that McKim, Mead & White designed, one was called the Appleton House, and it was built in Lenox, Massachusetts, in 1884 for Julia Amory Appleton. The second home was for John Cowdin. This commission was completed one year later, in 1885. The home was in a town called Far Rockaway, which is on Long Island, in New York.

Both homes have the butterfly floor plan that is seen in Wright's plan for the Cooper house. The room assignments and locations are different, and Wright's plan includes three wings, while the plans from the office of McKim, Mead & White only include two. All three homes have a main entry that opens onto a large hall that is then flanked by the wings of the house. Each home is designed with the dining room set to the rear of the house and to the left of center. Both the Appleton house and the Cowdin house would have had rooms separated by interior walls and doors, while Wright's design is open and has fewer closeable doorways. The exterior of the Appleton home was done in the Colonial Revival style, and the Cowdins' home, named Wave Crest, was done in the shingle style. Tragically, both houses were destroyed by fire. The Appleton home burned to the ground in 1905. Twelve years later, in 1917, the Cowdin home met the same fate when it, too, was consumed by a fire.

The story of the Cooper house plan does not lend itself to being categorized as a bootleg commission. It is unclear when or if Wright and Henry Cooper ever met to discuss this plan, and if they had met prior to the execution of Cooper's 1887 home, then the dates for any meetings do not coincide with the bootleg phase.

It has been documented that the dates of some of Wright's earlier works were less than exact. Wright has compounded the problem himself by adding notes or comments to completed drawings well after a plan was drawn up. The first drawing in the set of three Wright completed for the Cooper house plan has words written on the right-hand margin of the drawing; the two lines say:

> *Made while at U.W.*
> *Before going to Chicago 1885.*

Did Wright draw the prospective of the barn in 1885 and then use the same sheet to work out the placement of the proposed house? Drawing number 9004.001 does not mention Henry Cooper as a client, nor the village of La Grange as a location, while drawing number 9004.002 does include this information.

The preceding inventory numbers in the Frank Lloyd Wright archives are 9003 (unused), 9002 (the MacHarg House), and 9001 (Sullivan summer bungalow, Ocean Springs, Mississippi). Frank Lloyd Wright said he also designed the Charnleys' Ocean Springs, Mississippi summer home. Maybe at one time, the number 9003 was used for that project, but the house is not included in the Wright archives. Based on the sequencing of these inventory numbers, and with the Cooper plan being inventoried at number 9004, it follows that the plan was drawn up during the time Wright was employed at Adler & Sullivan. This project is not included in the catalog of work completed by Adler & Sullivan, as many of the buildings claimed by both parties were. As noted above, Wright and Cooper may have had contact prior to the 1890 date assigned to the drawing, but there is not enough evidence to clearly prove the relationship. Wright could have worked on the plan at his office or on his own time; there is no evidence for or against either choice. There is no verifiable proof that a contract was ever executed to create the necessary documentation for moonlighting to have taken place in respect to this project, and most importantly, a finished house was never completed. Therefore, this project is not being considered a bootleg design.

However, the plan is an important piece of Wright's early history because we can see how he is working out a scheme for a home from the initial sketch toward a finished design. We can see how Wright has proportioned each room so that it complements the adjoining spaces and how the parts contribute to the whole house. We can also see how Wright is beginning to create spaces that are defined less by actual walls and more by partitions and angles, and we see how he uses sight lines to draw a person's attention from one room into the next.

Since there are no drawings of the exterior elevations, we cannot know how much the house may have been influenced by Silsbee's or Sullivan's ideas.

In 1890, Wright did not complete any other commissions that are suspected to have been completed independently.

As noted above, the Chicago homes for George Blossom and Warren McArthur were numbered 9201 and 9203; the home that holds the identification number 9202 is the Robert G. Emmond home, which was constructed in La Grange, Illinois.

Robert G. Emmond Home

La Grange, Illinois, 1892

Whether Robert Emmond claimed his heritage as Scottish or English is not known, but his parents, Thomas and Jesse Emmond, were living in Melrose, Scotland, when he was born in 1850. Melrose is a ninety-minute train ride south of Edinburgh and about twelve miles north of the Scottish Borderlands. The River Tweed divides the city of Melrose as it flows through the countryside, heading toward the town of Berwick-upon-Tweed on the shores of the North Sea. During the twelfth century, King David I founded the Cistercian abbey in Melrose. This abbey, along with other abbeys from the surrounding area, became a center for sheep herding and the production of wool. The monks and their abbeys became victims of the wars between the Scots and the English, but the manufacturing of wool and woolen products stayed a constant in the area. In the 1800s, the many streams and rivers in and around Melrose fueled the transition of wool production

Robert Emmond house. Photographed by Douglas M. Steiner. *Courtesy of Douglas M. Steiner, Edmonds, WA.*

from individual farms into an industry that employed nearly 40 percent of Scotland's workforce by 1870. It is not known if Thomas or his son Robert were involved in the wool industry, but when Robert immigrated to the United States in the 1860s and settled in Chicago, he began working in the wholesale textile industry. On February 18, 1892, thirty-one-year-old Robert married twenty-five-year-old Alice Jones. After their wedding, they settled in Robert's hometown of Hinsdale, Illinois. Hinsdale is a suburb of Chicago that was founded in 1873 and lies about eighteen miles west of the city. The Chicago, Burlington & Quincy Railroad began providing passenger service for commuters from Hinsdale into the city as early as 1892.

The morning commuter trains pulled into Chicago's Union Station at Adams and Canal Street, and from there, it was a short walk for Robert to his office, which was listed in the 1892 Chicago directory as 211 West Jackson Boulevard. The dry goods commission firm of Jenkin & Kreer had offices at the same location. This firm dealt in both foreign and domestic textile products and was one of the few agencies buying fabric from Scotland in the 1880s. It could not be confirmed if Robert worked for Jenkin & Kreer, but it is quite plausible that he had business transactions with the firm. During the mid- to late 1800s, dry goods commission firms were established to function as the middlemen between the textile mills that manufactured cloth and the merchants who purchased the fabric to make clothing and other linen goods.

Robert and Alice had two children: a son, Wyatt, was born in July 1893, and their daughter, Margaret, was born two years later, in April 1895. The records do not say how, but Robert's wife, Alice, died just weeks after her daughter was born, on May 3, 1895. Robert never remarried and raised the children with help from his sister Agnes, who had immigrated to the United States from Scotland in 1899.

There is speculation that Robert and Frank Lloyd Wright may have met each other when Wright first arrived in Chicago. They may have stayed at the same hotel, or perhaps they met at some other location. In a 1988 interview with ninety-three-year-old Margaret (Emmond) Thompson, she told of how her father asked his friend Frank Wright to design their home in La Grange. After the home was finished, Wright would occasionally attend Sunday dinners at the Emmond home.

The home Wright designed for Robert and his family was located at 109 South Eighth Street in La Grange. There were no newspaper announcements for this new house, nor was there any need to disguise the architect, as it would be very unlikely that either of Wright's bosses would ever see or hear anything about this house. La Grange was a quiet farming town that was worlds away from the big city.

In Wright's early designs, he used different ideas and themes in combination with new concepts to see if these elements could be fused together. In the Emmond house, there are reminiscences of Silsbee's Queen Anne style, and the octagonal shapes from the Ocean Springs cottages are seen again in La Grange. A set of seven pages of construction blueprints for the Emmond house is held in the Frank Lloyd Wright archives. There have been alterations to Wright's original plan for the house; in fact, a major change happened soon after the home was built. The original blueprints show that both the main door and the side entrance are accessed after ascending six steps. In the drawing numbered 9202.001, both exterior stairways are uncovered. However, on sheet number 9202.006, the blueprint has hand-drawn lines showing two arched openings, one to each side of the main door, and a roofline is drawn from the arches back to the main roof. These lines are red in color, suggesting they were added after the original blueprint was published. We can assume that this side entrance was turned into a covered porch under Wright's supervision shortly after the Emmond family moved in. The main entry of the home is now quite visible, as it fronts Eighth Street. The home is set on a plot of land that is longer than it is wide. As we saw in the McArthur home, the more formal elevation faces toward the side of the lot. The front door faces west, allowing Wright to have the more detailed side of the house face south, and the rear of the building faces east, allowing the morning sun to shine into the living room. Originally, the entire exterior was sided with wooden clapboards. There are multiple roof sections covering various parts of the house. There are two octagonal towers, which set the dimensions of the interior rooms. The second-floor rooms include dormers cut into the roof and casement windows. The windows have large glass panels surrounded by a border that includes diamond pieces of transparent glass in caming.

The front door is arched in a similar fashion to the McArthurs', and on entering, there is a small reception hall on the same level as the threshold. Wright included a narrow band of trim at the top of the door that encircles the hall to give the effect of a large space. The stairs to the second floor are down the hall to the left of the entry, along with a built-in banquette bench and a decorative screen made from wooden spindles just above it. The stairway includes a long landing that is shielded by the screen and has a second bench, backed by two large windows that are set below a lunette window.

To the right of the entry door, one finds the reception room, which is spacious, with an outer wall that replicates the octagonal shape of the exterior; there are several windows that allow light to fill the room. On exiting the reception room, one enters the library, which has a fireplace in one corner and a set of doors that lead out to the covered porch. Originally, this space was an open terrace. Passing through the library into the living room, the second octagonal space is found. The outer wall includes just as many windows as the reception room did, but here, there are added sections of built-in seating to be found. One rectangular window has a diamond pattern throughout the field of glass; the other windows have diamond panes as a border, which encloses the center section of plain glass in the window. Since the room faces the backyard, the necessity for privacy is reduced.

The kitchen can be accessed from the entrance hall on one side or from the dining area on the opposite end of the house. The kitchen is open and has windows on two ends for light and ventilation.

The second floor has four bedrooms and a bathroom. Two of the bedrooms have the advantage of the increased size provided by the octagonal bays that rise from the first floor.

The Eammons' son, Wyatt, never married, and he lived with his parents until his death in 1936; his father, Robert, passed in 1939. Margaret was twenty-two when she married Kenneth Thompson in 1917, and on her father's death, she and her husband, who were still living in the family home, inherited the house. Margaret and Kenneth had two sons: Edmond, who was born in 1918, and Robert, who joined the family in 1924. Robert married and moved several times, living in Illinois, New York, and Connecticut; when he died, in 2014, he was living in Sarasota, Florida. Edmond, who stayed in Illinois, inherited the La Grange home after his parents died, and he lived there until 1993.

This home is another building that meets all the criteria for being from Wright's bootleg phase.

Margaret Thompson said in her family history that she knew Wright designed the house for her father before his wedding in 1893. Wright used the Queen Anne style as his inspiration for the home. There is no evidence that Robert Emmond had a relationship with either Dankmar Adler or Louis Sullivan, so this residential commission would not have come through the firm. Robert Emmond had a personal relationship with Wright, and Robert must have sought out his friend to design him a new home. Because of Wright's willingness to work out of his home studio on projects for Adler & Sullivan, he was able to move on to working on designs for his friends and acquaintances.

As Wright is working on his own commissions, he is beginning to establish a method of design that will allow him to create buildings that have distinctive rooms, as he has done in the Emmond house. He is also creating the essence of movement from one room to the next that is effortless. The views from one room to another allow us to feel we like are in a larger space, but at the same time, if we are sitting in either of the octagonal bays or near the inglenook, we are enclosed in a private space. Wright came to believe that the spaces enclosed by a building were just as important as the structure itself. For Wright, these spaces became the essence of the building.

The next commission found in the Wright archives is for another home in La Grange. This home is numbered 9209. This commission was for W. Irving Clark.

W. Irving Clark House

La Grange, Illinois, 1892

The Clark house has an odd history. There is no documentation to be found on how Clark and Frank Lloyd Wright may have met. Maybe there was a connection established through Wright's friendship with Robert Emmond; however, there is no firm evidence to support this theory.

In the roster of commissions done by Adler & Sullivan, the Clark house is not identified as one of their designs. The home is listed in the Frank Lloyd Wright archives and is identified as commission number 9209. The first advertisement for this home was published well after the house was completed and after Wright had left Adler & Sullivan's firm. The advertisement was seen in the *Inland Architect* volume 24, no. 1, dated August 1894, where a photogravure of the house along with the name of the architect was published. Since Wright had left the firm of Adler & Sullivan, there was no reason for him not to publicize one of his commissions, even if it was completed two years previously.

For the next forty-eight years, anyone who cared to research the lineage of this home would be able to find Wright's publication. However, in 1942, the certainty about the architect of this home was brought into question with the publication of Henry-Russel Hitchcock's book *In the Nature of Materials: The Buildings of Frank Lloyd Wright 1887–1941*. The copyright for this manuscript is held jointly by Frank Lloyd Wright (primary) and Henry-

W. Irving Clark house. *Courtesy of Douglas M. Steiner, Edmonds, WA.*

Russel Hitchcock (secondary). Hitchcock wrote under Wright's supervision when this book was produced. The work is divided into 6 parts, and part 6 includes a chronological list of Wright's work from 1887 through 1941. On the bottom of page 108, note 4 states the following:

> *The W. I. Clark house, 201 South La Grange Road, La Grange, Ill., was published as Wright's in the* Inland Architect *in 1894, vol. 24, no. I, but it was designed by E. Hill Turnock, an Adler and Sullivan draftsman. It is not clear how Wright's name came to be attached to it; but probably Turnock used Wright's name in announcing the commission.*

Did Frank Lloyd Wright use Hitchcock as his accomplice to denounce the Clark house design? As we scrutinize the account given in the paragraph above and review the design of this house as compared to other homes designed by Turnock, we will see that this little drama just may tell a different story than what was written by Hitchcock in 1942. There is also one surprising fact to be revealed that should clear up the question of who the architect for this house was.

By the time Hitchcock's book was published, Wright's bootleg career was well behind him. He had completed many of his grandest commissions by this time. He had redefined American residential architecture twice, first with Prairie-style homes and then with his designs for the Usonian homes. He had become internationally famous for both his work and his life. The question of who designed one house back in the 1890s was probably of little concern to the reviewers of this book when it was first published. An obscure comment in the notes section was hardly worth examining when the book also discussed Wright's masterpieces, like Unity Temple, the Robie house, the Imperial Hotel, and the Johnson Wax company's administration building.

However, if we look back to 1894, there were no retractions or corrections published in any of the following issues of the *Inland Architect* stating Turnock was the architect for this fine house. If Turnock were the architect, would he not have sought out such a retraction?

Turnock, who was born in London in 1872, grew up in Elkhart, Indiana, and made his way to Chicago in the 1880s. Once in Chicago, he went to work in the offices of William Lebron Jenney, not Adler & Sullivan. A notice in the July 1890 issue of the *Inland Architect*, in which Turnock announced he was opening his own independent office in Chicago, confirms this point.

Turnock was not as prolific a contributor to the *Inland Architect* as other more famous Chicago architects, but he did have pieces published in the journal, including in the photogravure edition. In the December 1892 issue of the *American Architect*, there was an announcement for a Chicago apartment building to be designed by Turnock. The article included the following statement (emphasis mine):

> *Mr. E. Hill Turnock is one of the leading architects of Chicago and has made not only the Jasper stone a special study, but also this kind of building.*

There are three points of concern with Hitchcock's statement about the W. Irving Clark house.

(1) If the work were Turnock's, why would he have waited until 1894 to "announce" the project when the home was built in 1892? The publishing of a photogravure would be reserved for a building that was already completed; it would not be used to announce the receiving of a commission, as many of the line drawings in the regular editions of the *Inland Architect* were used for.

(2) If Turnock was trying to link his own name to Wright's, as Hitchcock's statement implies, why would he not have ensured his name was printed next to Wright's on the photogravure? Additionally, Turnock was an established independent architect in 1892 and, based on the statement above, a rather good one. Why would he have tried to link his name to Frank Lloyd Wright's, who at this time was a relatively unknown Chicago "draftsman"?

(3) Given the expense of creating a photogravure, it seems unlikely that the publishers of this journal would mistakenly misname the architect of a completed home.

The house itself provides us with clues as to its designer. As has been noted earlier, when Wright was working on these independent commissions, he was experimenting with different historical styles and striving to find his own way to express his idea of what American architecture should be. This three-story house has nearly four thousand square feet of space, and it does not fit into a specific style but is a combination of the Queen Anne and shingle styles that Wright was familiar with. To be fair, Turnock would also have been familiar with these architectural styles.

The home sits on a large brick base, which Wright would turn into a concrete water table for his Prairie homes. The arched doorway, which is almost identical to the style of door seen in both the McArthur and Emmond houses, is achieved by ascending several steps to an open porch. There are two large bay windows to the right of the main entry; the bay is used to break the boxy effect of a plain, square house and to create the feeling of a larger room in the interior. The roof has a cross-axial design, not unlike the roof of Wright's own home, which he designed in 1889. The front gable has three oriel windows, one each for the front two bedrooms on the second floor and one in the third-floor recreation room. This third-floor window also has a half-round window above the oriel window. There are multiple dormers included to add light into the second-floor rooms and to give the rooms a larger feel. These are all features Wright was working with on his independent commissions.

In the original design, the master bedroom was situated in the front right-hand side of the second floor; the room had a fireplace, and it was connected to a nursery. A second fireplace was placed in the stairway hall. Today, the master bedroom is at the rear of the house and in the opposite corner. The room is connected to a large walk-in closet, a full washroom, and a laundry room. There is a second full bath off the central hall on the second floor and multiple closets, within each room and in the shared areas, also.

There is a fifth bedroom on the third floor that may have been used by a live-in housekeeper, as its size is utilitarian. There is a large storage room on the third floor along with over five hundred square feet of entertainment space.

On returning to the first floor, one will find that there is a small foyer flanked by the drawing room to the left and the reception room to the right. Both rooms are quite large; however, the reception room loses space to the fireplace. The floor plan has been altered over the years, so the sitting room, which was originally behind the reception room, is now a den that opens onto the screened porch. This room also has an adjoining bathroom, which is not original. The dining room was in the left rear corner of the home, as it still is today. The kitchen facilities are opposite the dining room. Today, the rear entrance has had a mud room added to the site with plenty of space for hanging coats and storing extra gear.

The primary stairway to the second floor is in its original location between the dining room and reception room. There is one handrail on the left side of the stairway, with a uniquely styled newel post at each landing. The posts have a Sullivanesque natural, leafy pattern carved into the finials. The stairway is a double L type, and there is a large, six-panel art glass window between the first and second landings. The three bottom windows are double hung, and the three upper windows are smaller and fixed in place. The colorful design includes stained glass in shades of green, white, and yellow, with curvilinear forms, ribbons, and a wreath. In the stairway hall is a second fireplace, creating two separate chimneys. Today, the first-floor rooms have been wallpapered; however, the walls would have been painted in the original design. The home was restored in 1988; the restoration architect was a man named John Thorpe. Thorpe was one of the primary individuals who took part in the restoration of Frank Lloyd Wright's Home and Studio. The kitchen was remodeled in 2012; the space was fully updated with appliances, new quartz countertops, and cabinetry.

The design of the roof, the blending of the interior spaces, the way the house is infused with light and shadow, the inclusion of natural spaces, the art glass windows, and the interior woodwork are all details that point to Wright's hand.

In 1893, Bjoerne Edwards, the publisher of the *American Contractor* journal, which was a rival to the *Inland Architect*, hired E. Hill Turnock to design a nine-story apartment building for him in the Lake View neighborhood of Chicago. The building was originally named Lincoln Park Palace but is now known as the Brewster Apartments. The building was appointed a Chicago landmark in 1982.

The exterior is constructed from pink jasper granite, and the stone faces are cut with a rusticated pattern. To say Turnock could not have designed two distinctively different buildings between 1892 and 1893 is not fair, but the Lincoln Park Palace would have taken more time and effort to design— and then to say he extended himself beyond his usual range of residential designs for the Clark house may be too much to consider.

Turnock returned to Elkhart in 1907 and designed several buildings there. The city of Elkhart offers an architectural tour of twelve of the buildings he designed. To say that any of these buildings resembles the Clark house is not possible. One of the mansions he designed was for Albert and Elizabeth Beardsley, which they named Ruthmere. This building is three stories, and Turnock designed the exterior using classic Beaux Arts features. This building has since been turned into a museum, which maintains a database of the buildings that Turnock designed, but by their own admission, the roster has not been academically verified. Even so, the Clark house is not included in the museum's catalog of Turnock's work. Conversely, the plans for the Clark house are in the Frank Lloyd Wright archives.

Those that know the history of Taliesin know that Wright's Wisconsin home has been rebuilt twice after experiencing devastating fires. The first fire was in 1914, when Julian Carlton, a member of the house staff, went on a murderous rampage, killing Wright's lover, Mamah Cheney, and her two children, Martha and John. Two of Wright's apprentices were also killed along with two local workers. Carlton then set the building ablaze and destroyed Wright's Wisconsin home. The second fire occurred on the evening of April

20, 1925; this fire took the home down again. Later, it was speculated that the fire may have been caused by lighting. These fires destroyed most of Wright's possessions, some personal papers, and several building construction blueprints. However, a bundle of drawings had been stuffed into a cubbyhole at the Taliesin studio building some time before 1914 and sat there untouched by either fire. This packet of drawings had long been forgotten about until 1967, when, during an effort to reorganize the space, the bundle was pulled out and the Clark house drawings completed by Frank Lloyd Wright were rediscovered. Other drawings from the 1890s that were exhumed at that time included Wright's 1896 designs for the unbuilt Screw Factory building for a client and family friend named Charles E. Roberts. Two sets of drawings for Madison boathouses from 1893 were included in this cache, along with an original pen-and-ink drawing of Wright's submittal for the Milwaukee Public Library and Museum design competition, which was also held in 1893.

This collection of drawings suggests that the lineage of the Clark house begins with the hand of Frank Lloyd Wright. Why would Hitchcock have started his misleading story? Hitchcock penned a letter, which was published in the July–August 1978 issue of the Frank Lloyd Wright Foundation's newsletter, that attempts to clarify his earlier comments. In the letter, he suggests for the first time that "after the drawings were completed there was a break between Wright and the Clarks." He further suggests that it was the Clarks who may have sought out Turnock to supervise the construction. To distance himself from the controversy, Hitchcock further states:

> He [meaning Wright] *usually denied, as he did to me in this case, the authorship of works on which he did not control the supervision.*

Here again we find Hitchcock citing a fact that even Wright contradicts. It was common for Wright not to supervise the construction of the bootleg houses, because he was working during the day at Adler & Sullivan. Wright even refers to the lack of supervision on these independent projects in his autobiography when he says:

> *I did not try anything radical because I could not follow up on them.*

So, the comment about Wright denying authorship because he did not supervise the construction does not seem to hold water. The break between the Clarks and Wright is also hard to defend because there is no documentation to support or deny the claim. Also, there is little information known about Clark or his family other than that his father was a building contractor, he was married, and he was an attorney who worked out of his home. According to his obituary, which was published in the *Chicago Tribune* on December 14, 1895, after his death on December 12, he left behind his wife, Louise, and four children, Irving, George, Ella, and Palmer.

If Wright tried to disown this house, why would he have waited so long to do so? The answer just might not ever be known. Perhaps in a future remodeling project at Taliesin, more documentation will be uncovered that provides an explanation for this mystery.

Now, knowing that Wright designed this house and reviewing all the information presented, we can list this commission as a bootleg design. The commission checks several of the boxes from the list of criteria; there is no known relationship between the Clarks and the firm of Adler & Sullivan; and the building has never been claimed by anyone to have been designed by that firm.

Wright did not try to conceal his authorship of the house for the same reasons as the Emmond house. Covert work on the original plans would have been completed in Wright's home office. Finally, even though there is little information known about the Clarks, by all accounts, they were the client for this project.

The last commission from La Grange was for a man named Peter Goan, who had his house completed by Wright. Peter's son Orin also sought out Wright to design him and his wife a home on a lot adjacent to Emmond's home. However, Orin's home became an unrealized commission. These projects also bring up issues with the dating of Wright's early work. The Peter Goan house has been alternatively dated to 1893 and 1894; the project number assigned to this design by the Frank Lloyd Wright archives is 9403, suggesting the work was done in 1894. The Orin Goan project was assigned the number 9406, and since the home was not constructed using Wright's plans, we can be sure that this number only denotes the date of the original design.

Peter Goan House

La Grange, Illinois, 1894

The Peter Goan house was built directly across the street from the Emmond house, so it is likely that Peter Goan chose Wright as his architect based on a recommendation from his neighbor.

Peter Goan was born in 1832 in Somerset County in southwestern Pennsylvania, where he and his three siblings were raised. As a young man, Peter gravitated toward building construction, which he found to his liking. He apprenticed with a local carpenter to learn the trade. Whether it was for work or because of wanderlust, Peter made his way west in the early 1850s. In 1855, Peter married Emily J. Cain in Dubuque County, Iowa, and by 1860, Peter is listed in the Dubuque City address directory as a woodworking superintendent. Peter must have been well thought of, because an 1880 publication on the history of Dubuque County, Iowa, includes a short biography of him and his family. During their time in Dubuque, Peter and Emily must have been happily married, because together they had seven children.

By 1887, Peter, who had turned fifty-five, had moved to Chicago. His name appears in the 1889 voter registration ledger. As Peter was getting older, he must have been looking to move out of the city and find a quieter location to settle down once he had the chance to retire, and he found himself heading to La Grange, Illinois. He and his wife and two of their children are listed in the 1900 federal census as living in Lyons Township, Cook County, in Illinois. The village of La Grange is located within this area.

For the design of the roof on the Peter Goan house, Wright used a simple hip roof with dormers on multiple sides. The house also has two projecting bays to extend the size of the rooms. Wright was using both design elements in other bootleg houses, too. The front room bay is one floor high, while the dining room bay extends to the second floor but does not protrude through the rooftop. The wide and deep front porch Wright included in the original design was removed. Wright used a brick foundation for the base of the house and wood battens for the first-floor exterior. This wood treatment continues up past the ceiling level of the first floor to the sills of the second-floor windows. The remainder of the exterior walls are finished with stucco.

The plans Wright created show the first floor to have an open feel. On entering the front door, you would walk into a small vestibule, which opened into the reception hall. The large, open living room is stationed to the left, and this room connects to the dining room through an open doorway. The living room includes a very intimate inglenook. The dining room includes built-in cabinetry designed by Wright. At the rear of the house, a large kitchen is placed next to the pantry, which separates the kitchen from the dining room. Beside the pantry, there is another area for storage at the rear of the house where the back door is found. The stairs to the second floor are placed between the reception hall and the

Peter Goan house. *Courtesy of Douglas M. Steiner, Edmonds, WA.*

kitchen. This location moves the stairs away from being a focal point, like one might see in a more grandiose house. The second floor is laid out very simply, with four chamber rooms and a bath. The two front chamber rooms are mirror images of each other. The room that is in the left rear of the house is made a little larger because of the bay wall that rises from the first floor. An interesting note is that Wright added a message on the plans to inform the builder that the roof that covered the first-floor porch was to be made of tin. Therefore, it is unlikely that this area was intended to be an accessible balcony, as there are no exit doors to this space from either of the two front bedrooms. Also, such a roof would be difficult to walk on because the material would be hot in the summer and slippery in the rainy weather.

Peter and his wife continued to live in the Wright-designed home until Peter passed away in 1911.

For the construction of the Peter Goan house, Wright created eight plan sheets. These sheets are numbered 9403.001 through 9403.008. These plan sheets do not include any dates, and Wright did not list an office location where the drawings might have been drawn up.

The numbering of the drawings is our first clue as to their heritage: with the first two digits being 94, we must believe they were made in 1894. This places the house outside of Wright's bootleg period. It has been suggested that the 1894 date is derived from the date of the finished construction of the home. It has also been suggested that the styling of the home is too unimaginative to have come after the Winslow house, which was designed in 1893. The Winslow house can be considered one of Wright's early masterpieces. And the Peter Goan home was designed and built after Wright left Adler & Sullivan.

Wright worked on twelve commissions during 1894, and only two of them were influenced by the Winslow house. Both projects came later in the year, as their project numbers were 9406 and 9407, respectively. None of the commissions between numbers 9401 and 9405 show any similarities to the Winslow house. Thus, assuming that the Peter Goan plan sheets are misdated and then classifying the house as a bootleg project simply because it was not inspired by the Winslow house makes for a weak argument.

Because the Peter Goan house is numbered 9403, I believe that it should not be designated as a bootleg house.

To find the remaining homes that have been proposed to have been from Wright's bootleg phase, we will need to visit Wright's hometown of Oak Park, Illinois. The homes that will be discussed are all located within a leisurely walk from Wright's home at 951 Chicago Avenue.

The Oak Park Homes

So long as we had the luxuries, the necessities could pretty well take care of themselves.
—Frank Lloyd Wright, speaking of family life

Thomas H. Gale and Robert P. Parker Homes

Oak Park, Illinois, 1892

Thomas Gale was a real estate developer, and he owned several vacant lots in the residential section of Oak Park. On two of these lots, he commissioned Frank Lloyd Wright to build two homes. Gale's home still bears his name as the original owner; the second house became known as the Robert P. Parker home. The inventory numbers in the Wright archives for these two homes are 9203 and 9206, respectively.

The story of how Thomas Gale came to reside in Oak Park, Illinois, starts in the early 1800s, when the United States Congress passed legislation that created the Illinois Territory in 1809. Illinois achieved statehood in 1818, and the state started attracting homesteaders and shop owners. The Blackhawk

War of 1832 slowed settlement in the north, but land sales recovered quickly after 1834. The state was a welcoming place, so much so that a carpenter from Kentucky named Thomas Lincoln moved his wife and six children from Elizabethtown, Kentucky, to Decatur, Illinois, in 1830. The Lincoln family's oldest son, Abraham, would go on to become an attorney, a statesman, and, eventually, the president of the United States.

The dream of owning one's own farm must have been compelling for the likes of forty-year-old Abram Gale and his wife, Sarah, who left their home state of New York in 1835 and traveled west with their three children, Georgianna (birthdate unknown) and their two sons, Edwin (three years old) and William (one year old). On arriving in the small farming community west of Chicago called Jefferson, Abram purchased 320 acres of premium farmland. In time, the community's name of Jefferson faded away, and the area where Abram's farmland was developed became known as Galewood. This Chicago neighborhood still bears the Galewood moniker. The area shares its southern border with the village of Oak Park today.

The boys, Edwin and William, prospered in their new home, and Abram and Sarah welcomed their fourth child, Sally, in 1896. In 1849, the

Opposite: Thomas H. Gale house. *Courtesy of Douglas M. Steiner, Edmonds, WA.*

Right: Robert P. Parker house. *Courtesy of Douglas M. Steiner, Edmonds, WA.*

Gale boys became apprentices to Henry Bowman, who owned a drugstore in Chicago. In 1856, these industrious young men purchased their own drugstore, and in 1859, they took on a partner named William Blocki. Eventually, the partnership grew to include six drugstores throughout Chicago and a seventh in Oak Park. During this period of growth, these young businessmen began importing and distributing bottled water, which was often prescribed as a treatment for stomach problems caused by the unhealthy City of Chicago water.

At the outbreak of the American Civil War in 1861, William Gale was of draft age; however, he volunteered to join the Union army. He was assigned to the Chicago Board of Trade Battery, Illinois Light Artillery Division. Edwin, who was twenty-nine years old and had a wife and three children, did not volunteer, and no service records are listed for him. One of the first major battles that the Illinois Light Artillery Division participated in was the Stone's River Battle, which took place near Murfreesboro, Tennessee; the battle began on New Year's Eve 1862 and ended on January 5 with a Union victory. During the battle, William was severely wounded; however, when he recovered, he continued to serve in the Union army by taking on the position of quartermaster. On William's return home at the end of the war, his battle-weary body needed rest more than it did work, and he retired from the drugstore business.

The Gale and Blocki enterprise grew, and with the inescapable bouts of waterborne diseases affecting Chicagoans, such as cholera, dysentery, and typhoid fever, their bottled water business was becoming more popular.

In 1882, Edwin and William purchased a Wisconsin-based water-bottling company called the White Rock Water Company. The business became very successful due to its distributing their products nationally.

In the 1850s, Edwin had met Julia Hart while she was attending school in Chicago; they were married in 1856. The Gale family continued to prosper, and in 1860, Edwin built an expansive Gothic Revival–style home in Oak Park, while Blocki had an Italianate home built in Oak Park's neighboring suburb to the west named River Forest. Edwin and Julia were blessed with seven sons; the oldest, Oscar, was born in 1858, and their youngest, Oliver, arrived in 1887. Their middle son, Thomas, was born in 1866. Thomas lived his entire life in Oak Park; he was an attorney and developed a successful real estate business that, according to the Chicago papers, dealt in land and home sales and provided rental properties, as well. He was active in Oak Park's social circles and was elected president of the Oak Park cycling club in 1892. He was also an active member of the Unitarian Church of Oak Park. Thomas had met Laura Robeson, who hailed from Port Huron, Michigan, while they both were attending the University of Michigan in Ann Arbor. Laura was a popular girl; the local newspaper, the *Port Huron Daily Times*, reported on her travels to and from Canada. The *Daily Times* also reported when the couple's wedding invitations were sent out and on the wedding itself.

In 1891, Thomas and Laura were married and chose to live in Oak Park, where Laura quickly found her way into the social scene by becoming a member of the drama club and the prominent Nineteenth Century Club. Frank Lloyd Wright was affiliated with the Unitarian Church of Oak Park, and Wright's wife, Catherine, was also a member of the Nineteenth Century Club. These two young couples were part of the same social circle. In 1892, when the Gales were looking for a new home, they chose Frank Lloyd Wright as their architect. Thomas Gale also played a role in one of Wright's greatest achievements: he owned the property that he eventually sold to the Unitarian congregation for Unity Temple in 1905.

Edwin Gale (Thomas's father) had bought a large tract of land in Oak Park that was fronted by Chicago Avenue. The land was eventually divided into lots that were just over one-quarter of an acre. These lots were narrow but very deep. Edwin sold this land to his son Thomas, who in turn sold all but two lots. Thomas commissioned Wright to design two homes for these lots. Thomas and his family would live in one of the homes, and the other was built on speculation. Whether Thomas knew attorney Robert Parker professionally or by another association is not known. Parker must have become aware of the land/house sale soon after the offer was advertised, because Parker's name is on the original house plans Wright created for this site. Parker, who was living on North Clark Street in Chicago prior to moving to Oak Park, must have had a productive law practice; news of his cases was regularly published in the Chicago papers. Other than these few facts, little else is known about Parker's personal life.

The two homes that Wright had designed date from 1892, which was a busy year for Wright. Not only was he gaining more independence in his position with Adler & Sullivan, but he and Catherine also welcomed their second child, John Lloyd Wright, into their family.

Wright based the plan of the two houses Gale had commissioned on the design of the Emmond home from earlier in the year. Wright was honoring his first employer, Joseph Lyman Silsbee, by using the Queen Anne style as the foundation for these designs.

Wright's own home was at the corner of Forest and Chicago Avenues; the Gale and Parker homes are a short walk west from that intersection. Both homes are on the south side of Chicago Avenue. The Emmond home was on a large lot in a rural suburb that could accept a large home with a tall, angular roof and generously sized towers. The Oak Park homes were on narrow urban lots, so Wright reduced the width and the depth of each house. These homes have only two towers, which are in line with each other, so the rear tower is blocked from the street view by the front tower. The towers on each house rise from the foundation of the house and extend to the second floor. The towers have an octagonal shape, as seen in other works of Wright during this early phase of his career.

Each tower is covered by a steep roof that mirrors the tower's profile. The roof merges with the main hip roof that covers the rest of each home. Wright embellishes the roof with geometric dormers that have casement windows that would allow light into the second-floor rooms and could be opened to allow the warm summer air to escape the living quarters. In other bootleg homes, Wright experimented with placing the main entry to the side of the house; these two Oak Park homes have the main entry facing the street side elevation, and the doors are not concealed but are easily attained by a walkway that leads directly to the front door from the public sidewalk. The door to the Emmond house is arched, while both Oak Park homes have typical rectangular doorways.

One of the distinguishing features of Wright's Prairie houses was the accentuation of the horizontal line. Wright used traditional narrow clapboard siding to show this horizontal effect on these homes at a point early in his career. The parallel lines of the boards force our eyes to see around the house, and this horizontality counters the vertical pitch of the roofs.

The floor plans of both the Gale and Parker houses are similar. On entry, one is welcomed into a small foyer, with the second-floor stairs directly to the right; both homes have benches at the base of the stairway, and each seat has an architecturally pleasant wooden wall with three horizontal panels placed symmetrically above the bench. The walls are topped with a spindle framed screen to allow light into the staircase that rises behind the wall. The first three steps are wide and stop at a large, well-lit landing, which would allow for easy movement up or down the staircase. Neither of the stairways have handrails included, but Wright did create an extremely tall newel post to adorn each of these spaces.

The floor plan Wright devised had the reception room located in the front tower, which would have been followed by a library; the dining room followed and would be placed in the rear tower. The kitchen was behind the staircase, and a pantry and porch would be situated behind the kitchen to the rear of the house. Each kitchen included a full wall of built-in cabinets, drawers, and shelves for ample storage. The second-floor spaces in both homes are divided into four bedrooms and a full bathroom.

The two larger bedrooms are above the reception room and then the dining room. These rooms are in the upper sections of the towers and have wraparound windows for a pleasant view and a wide-open feel to each room. Two smaller bedrooms are on the opposite side of the second floor and are lit by dormer windows. During the first decade of the Gales' time in their Wright-designed house, they welcomed two children, named Sarah and Edwin.

After the beginning of the twentieth century, the Gales began to consider the idea of a new house. They contacted their architect and friend Frank Lloyd Wright and asked him to work up a plan. Wright was well into his Prairie period by this time, so their new home was to be quite different than their first house. Wright prepared a set of presentation drawings for the Gales in 1904, but unfortunately, after they were completed, Thomas became quite ill. It became Laura's duty to care for him as he was stricken with cancer, and the new house plans were put on hold. The following year came with more sad news for the family, as the child Laura was carrying died on the very same day he was born. Laura lovingly cared for her husband as best she could, but in 1907, Thomas finally succumbed to his disease.

As Wright's family was expanding, you might say his financial situation was shrinking. His continual need for more revenue was ever prevalent throughout his career.

These two bootleg houses were hastily designed, and Wright made little effort to significantly change the plans he had used in the Emmond house. But these houses also meet the criteria of being bootleg commissions, as they were designed well within the time frame of Wright's bootleg phase. The Gales and the Wrights were neighbors and friends, so they must have had few qualms about accepting house plans written up by Wright in his home studio. With Wright living in Oak Park, there would have been no reason for Thomas to see him at his downtown office. The commission would have been agreed to by a handshake either in Wright's home office or as they sat in the cozy inglenook next to the hearth in Wright's home.

Another person Wright had both a personal and a professional relationship with was a fellow Oak Parker named Charles E. Roberts. The first commission for Roberts ended up being an unbuilt project, but this was not the last commission worked on by these two men. The unbuilt plan has the number 9210, which places this work well within Wright's bootleg phase. But can it be cataloged as one of Wright's bootleg commissions?

Charles E. Roberts Project

Oak Park, Illinois, 1892

The Roberts family moved to Oak Park in 1885 and had a custom house designed by another notable Chicago architectural firm, Burnham & Root. Daniel H. Burnham and his partner, John W. Root, became successful Chicago architects while Wright was still in his teens. Root was only twenty-one years old when, in 1871, he took on the position of draftsman in the firm of Carter, Drake and Wright.

One year later, twenty-six-year-old Daniel Burnham joined the same firm, and in 1873, these two men began their own company. Twenty years later, Burnham was offering a young draftsman who, at the time, was still employed by Adler & Sullivan a position at his firm, an offer that included not only a highly sought-after station but also an all-expenses-paid scholarship to complete six years of education. This young man was none other than Frank Lloyd Wright. Wright referred to Burnham as Uncle Dan. He explained in his autobiography that not only did Uncle Dan's offer include the scholarship to study in France at the École des Beaux-Arts, but also, on completion of the curriculum, he would be able to continue his studies in Rome, Italy, at the American Academy. Wright turned down this generous offer; with a wife and child at home and a burning desire to begin his own independent career, he could not afford to leave home for that long a period.

By 1887, Wright's mother, Anna, must have been getting anxious about not being able to see her son as often as she would have wished for. So, she packed up her belongings and, with her two daughters in tow, moved to Chicago. Anna first settled in on the north side of the city but did not find the area to her liking. She was unwilling to move to the far south side for fear that her overbearing brother, the pastor Jenkin Lloyd Jones, would be too controlling. Anna had been managing her own affairs without any interference for the past seven years since her divorce from William. However, her brother Jenkin did suggest she accept lodging with the Unitarian reverend, named Augusta Chapman, who was living in Oak Park. This arrangement suited Anna's needs. As she was getting settled into Chapman's home, another boarder joined them: Wright himself moved in. Anna's family of three children were back together again. Reverend Chapman and her four boarders would head dutifully to Sunday services at Unity Church in Oak Park, and this is where Wright first came to know Charles E. Roberts.

Roberts was one of the officers of the Standard Screw Company, and in 1894, he received a patent for a screw-manufacturing machine. This new machine reduced production costs by 40 percent and eventually allowed the company to reduce prices for its new automobile-manufacturing customers. This was not the only invention created by Roberts; after the screw machine, he received other patents, too, including a drive wheel for motorcycles, an internal expanding brake, and, lastly, his design of his own automobile. When Wright bought his property on Chicago Avenue, Roberts lived about three blocks east, on Euclid Avenue.

The first project these two friends worked on was a sketch Wright worked up in 1892, during the height of his bootleg career. Roberts, besides being a businessman and inventor, was also a land developer.

The house Wright designed had two stories and a hip roof. The home had a front porch and a driveway that was curved like a horseshoe. The exterior was covered in clapboard siding. The second-floor windows terminated just under the outreaching eaves. The placement of the windows was high on the interior walls, allowing for privacy from the street. We can also see that there was a chimney placed near the center of the front-facing roof panel. The chimney would have serviced two adjoining fireplaces. The living room hearth is set into a corner, and the adjoining parlor's fireplace is built into the corner of that room on the opposite side of the wall.

Wright completed a set of four drawings for this project. The first two sheets hold pencil sketches and are not detailed drawings. The remaining sheets show the complete room layouts for both the first and second floors.

Even though the plan for the unbuilt Cooper house has been reviewed by other authors, the plan for the unbuilt Charles Roberts house is rarely spoken of. Maybe the uniqueness of the Cooper plan or the opportunity to highlight how Wright was influenced by others besides Silsbee and Sullivan is why we see that project discussed so often.

The plans for the Roberts house were not influenced by another architect's work. These plans show, again, that Wright is moving away from Silsbee's Queen Anne style and developing his own idea for the horizontality of the exteriors of his buildings' designs. Wright is also purposely stating his desire for an open floor plan by including the phrase "No Doors" on the plans near the walls and openings that separate the dining room and reception hall from the parlor. He is also fleshing out his ideas for a path of discovery: to make your way from the front door, two perfect right-angle turns and a rise of seven steps would need to be traversed to arrive in the reception hall. Another curious thing about the third and fourth drawings is the handwriting Wright used to make the notations of room names and the built-in seat in the reception hall. The text is playful; the first letter of each word is oversized and includes decorative serif points to accentuate the letters. The text for the title of the drawing is so mischievous that you cannot help but smile while you are reading the words. The lettering could be described as an Art Deco design, but this style of design would not officially begin to be recognized until years later.

The period of these plans is well within the time frame of Wright's bootleg phase. The client was a close family friend of Wright's, so the project was not assigned by his firm. And since Wright would likely not have worked on these designs as he was sitting in the office next to Sullivan's, he certainly would have done them in his home studio. If the archives only contained one sketch that did not include construction details, it could be surmised that Wright was doing his friend Charles a favor by giving him an idea for what a new home might look like. But that is not the case. Wright developed four plan sheets, and two of these are detailed. Wright must have spent more than a few hours working on these drawings. The key question would be: Did Charles Roberts pay a fee for these drawings? If even a verbal contract existed, these drawings would become part of a commission. It is very plausible that Wright did in fact charge a fee for these drawings. Why the project was not completed is unknown, but Wright's work up to the point of the last two drawings must be considered moonlighting. Unlike the Cooper house project, where no client may have existed, this project includes all the necessary criteria for a bootleg project: there was a client, a contract would have existed, Wright solicited the work on his own, and the drawings were completed outside of Wright's office hours.

However, no house was built, and the quest we are on is to find Wright's bootleg houses. So, even though the first four criteria were met, the fact that no house was built means this project cannot be labeled a bootleg house. The other projects Wright and Roberts worked on were all dated post-1894 and well after Wright's bootleg phase was over.

As 1892 is ending, determining if the remaining projects Wright may have completed before he left Adler & Sullivan should be classified as belonging to his bootleg phase becomes difficult because of three criteria: the date of the building's design, the date of final construction, and the date when Wright left Adler & Sullivan.

The Frank Lloyd Wright archives list six commissions in the year 1893: one commission was for an unbuilt project, and another was for two separate commercial buildings, of which only one was built. The remaining built commissions cause some difficulty in figuring out their sequence of appearance during the year. We will review these commissions and try to determine their place in the order of the other bootleg projects.

Thomas Gale's older brother Walter also owned a vacant lot on Chicago Avenue. His lot was directly next door, to the west of his brother's home. Walter had followed his father into the family drugstore business. Walter must have found the design of his brother's home to his liking, or he thought: If Wright was the neighborhood architect, then why not have him design his house? So, at number 9302 in the archives, we find the Walter Gale house.

Walter H. Gale House

Oak Park, Illinois, 1893

Cora Gookins was born in Wisconsin during the summer of 1863. She was the only child of William and Adeline Gookins, who had settled in Oak Park in 1866. Cora met Walter Gale, and they married in 1884.

Walter was an active member of Unity Church, where he and Cora met Frank and Catherine Wright. Walter and Cora were prominent, but not ostentatious, members of the community. Notices of the couple's travels to the East Coast and Walter's activities in both the Professional Pharmacists Association and the National Association of Retail Druggists could be found in the Chicago-area papers, but you did not see their names in the society pages.

The house Wright designed for Walter and Cora has some of the same characteristics as the Thomas Gale and the Robert Parker homes. This home dates to 1893 and has the inventory number 9302, suggesting the home was designed early in the year. However, it is difficult to determine when the design was completed versus when the construction was finished.

The Sunday real estate edition of the *Inter Ocean* newspaper on October 29, 1893, included a short article which stated that Frank Lloyd Wright was designing a two-story home on Chicago Avenue in Oak Park. This fact leads us to believe the plans were drawn up in the fall of 1893, after Wright had left the firm of Adler & Sullivan.

Wright created seven plan sheets that have survived and are in the Frank Lloyd Wright archives. These plans are not dated, and there is no evidence that they were completed in Wright's Schiller Building offices. The plans were most likely drawn up in Wright's home studio.

The design is another rendition of a Queen Anne home. The Walter Gale house is a two-story home, and the roof is of a large gable design; the long axis of the roof faces the front elevation. A rectangular open porch extends down the west side of the house where the main entry door is. There are two other features that stand out on the front facade. There is a large, two-story conical tower and an overly tall rectangular dormer that rises from the roof to the left side of the tower. The flowing lines of the roof are broken by a tall brick chimney on the east side of the house. There is one fireplace that was in a room that was labeled as a library on the original plans. There is another fireplace in the dining room, and its chimney can just be seen poking above the peak of the roof.

The conical tower's perpendicular roof is a complex design that includes a traditional gable rake structure extending from the main roof, but instead of a flat gable end panel, Wright has the roof follow the conical pattern of the tower. The lower portion of the roof is flared out so the extended eaves can shed rainwater out and over the edge of the roof. During Wright's career, roofs would no longer be just protective covers for a building; they would become integrated design features that help extend horizontal lines

Walter H. Gale house. *Courtesy of Douglas M. Steiner, Edmonds, WA.*

and supply a purpose for other cantilever assemblies to break up the boxy look of an ordinary house.

There are three large, rectangular double-hung windows on the first floor of the tower and a banded set of casement windows in the upper portion. The second-floor windows have a lead came diamond pattern, while the lower set only includes the diamond pattern in the upper portion of the window.

At the base of the dormer is a double-hung window with plain transparent glass, and the upper window is a casement style with a came diamond pattern. Between the windows is a decorative wood festoon wreath.

The two side end gables walls were designed by Wright to be three separate panels; not only does this break up the monotony of a large, flat wall, but the top and middle wall sections also have a flared course of shingles at the lower edge designed to shed water away from the wall below.

Wright uses design elements on the exterior that are from the Queen Anne period, but then he creates his own scheme to break away from a strict interpretation of that style and creates something unique.

On entering the Walter Gale house, the reception room is directly to your left at the base of the tower. The library adjoins the main hall at the front of the house. In the hall, the stairs to the second floor can be found on the right-hand side, and one of the doorways to the dining room is ahead on the left. At the far end of the hall is a door to a hallway that leads to the kitchen. There is a second doorway to the dining room that allows access to the pantry.

The second floor has four bedrooms. The primary bedroom room is in the tower, and there are two large bedrooms to the left of the main room. One is above the library, and the second is above the dining room. The bathroom and the servant's room are to the rear of the second floor. The two front bedrooms have ample closet space, and the master bedroom has a walk-in dressing room.

The Chicago Directory Company published the *Chicago Blue Book of Selected Names for Chicago and Suburbs* from 1885 until 1915. Walter and Thomas Gale's names and addresses were published in these directories as early as 1890 and continued to be listed until 1905 and 1907, respectively. Each book was printed in December for the upcoming year, meaning that the information in these books had to be compiled in the fall so that it could be published prior to the start of the year. Therefore, another clue for when the Walter H. Gale house was built can be inferred from this information. In the 1893 and 1894 editions of the Chicago Blue Book, Walter's address is listed in the Austin neighborhood of Oak Park, while the 1895 edition has him listed on Chicago Avenue. If Walter and his wife had moved into their house in early 1893, his address information in the 1894 directory would have reflected this. Conversely, if their move-in date came after the publishing deadline, their current address would not be published until 1895. This is likely what happened.

In 1910, Walter and Cora were still living in Oak Park, but by this time, Cora's older brother George, who was a teacher, and his wife and children were also living at the same address.

Sometime after 1910, Cora's mother, her brother, and his family moved to Los Angeles, California. In 1916, Walter and Cora were spending the winter with them. In February, Walter was called back to Oak Park to deal with some business affairs. Walter seemed to be in good health on his return, but he began to feel ill, and by mid-March, he was checked into a local hospital. Instead of getting better, Walter's condition worsened, and he passed away on March 23, 1916. Afterward, Cora moved permanently to live with her brother's family in Los Angeles, until her death in 1923.

It is well documented that by the fall of 1893, Wright had left Adler & Sullivan and was sharing office space with Cecil Corwin in the Schiller Building. He may have also been working out of his own home studio. After leaving Adler & Sullivan, Wright was not instantly busy; he would have had sufficient available time to work on these drawings to have completed them prior to the newspaper notice for the Walter Gale house on October 29.

With a construction date for the Walter Gale house in November 1893, the design of the home would be outside the parameters of the bootleg phase. Therefore, this home is not being counted as a bootleg design.

The last home in Oak Park to be discussed is another home that is walking distance from Wright's home studio. This home is another commission that has been linked to Wright's bootleg phase, but there is uncertainty about its lineage. The archives have assigned it the number 9405, but the home dates to the year 1893.

Francis J. Woolley House

Oak Park, Illinois, 1893

Francis Woolley was born in Milwaukee, and in 1887, he graduated from the University of Michigan with a degree in philosophy. After graduating, he moved to the city of Chicago, where he was able to pass the Illinois bar exam and became a practicing attorney. In 1892, he married Cora Belle Low, and by 1893, the couple was listed as living at 6625 Wright Street in Chicago. In the Lakeside directory of 1894, the couple's home address was listed only as Oak Park; there was no street name or address number included.

The commissions Wright completed after he left Adler & Sullivan were done quickly. In Wright's haste, he misspelled the Woolleys' name on the drawings by dropping the second *L* in their last name. Or Wright may have decided that it was time for the Woolleys to have a surname that followed the spelling rules for U.S. English, rather than the British instructions, which required two *L*s.

When Wright left Adler & Sullivan, he was either brave or foolish to walk out on the firm that was providing him with a weekly paycheck. Now, his income would be produced from fees for service. The commission for the Woolley house might have just kept the ever-present bill collectors at bay.

Francis and Cora must have been an unassuming couple, because other than an occasional mention of Francis's legal cases in the *Chicago Tribune*, little

Francis J. Woolley house. Photographed by Douglas M. Steiner. *Courtesy of Douglas M. Steiner, Edmonds, WA.*

is known about them. They did have two children: a son, Francis L. Woolley Jr., born in 1896, and a daughter, Alice, who came along two years later. The couple's names were not published in the society pages, and they were not listed in the Chicago Blue Book until 1897. The home Wright designed for them was the fourth of the Oak Park modified Queen Anne–style homes he designed between 1892 and 1893. Wright employed the use of multiple bays to extend rooms, as he had done in other recent commissions. The house does not have the dominant tower feature like the houses for the Gales and Robert Parker. The hip roof does have multiple dormer windows. The bays begin at the top of the foundation and rise to the eaves but do not protrude through the roof.

The front entry door is easily recognizable, as it is centered on a front porch that is covered by another traditional hip roof, which is supported by columns. These columns are fabricated from brick-and-mortar bases with wood-framed capitals. The home does include a basement, which was needed for the utilities. Originally, Wright specified lap board siding that began just above the foundation and continued to the sills of the second-floor windows. At this point, there was a horizontal wood band, which was used as a break between the lap board and the shingled siding that was installed from here to the eaves. The hip roof does not extend any farther than what you might see on any other house on the block.

From the original blueprints, you can imagine the house and how it would have looked when the Woolleys moved in. Stepping through the front door, they would have walked into the reception hall. From this area, they would have been able to see down a long hall, bypassing the stairway to the second floor, to the space where the kitchen would be. To their right was the parlor, where the first large bay was, and to their left, there was a wide opening in the wall that led to the library, where the second bay was located, along with a cozy fireplace tucked into the southeast corner of the room. Beyond the library was the dining room. The kitchen had access to the dining room and the last of the bayed walls was here at the back of the house. The second floor held four bedrooms and the washroom. The master bedroom was a large room at the front of the house and assumed the space of both the reception hall and the parlor below. Another large bedroom was over the library and included another fireplace, followed by two bedrooms that were sized for the children: one was located over the kitchen and the other over the dining room. The bay structure from the first-floor dining room was not extended to this second-floor bedroom. The house was a very straightforward, affordable design.

Francis and his wife, Cora, moved to Glencoe, Illinois, in 1904, and by 1925, they were living in Evanston, Illinois, where Francis passed away in 1928. Cora remained in Evanston until her death twelve years later, in 1940. According to Francis's obituary, he had been in court on Tuesday, December 11, but on Friday the fourteenth, he died suddenly at sixty-three years of age. Cora's obituary said she passed away at her home at seventy-five.

The Woolley house has been listed as one of Wright's bootleg commissions by some researchers. This may be because of the design of the home and not because of the period in which it was commissioned. This house gives us another opportunity to try to see how the dating of Wright's work can cause confusion. In the Frank Lloyd Wright archives, the number 9405 is assigned to the Woolley house. As was explained earlier, the archives' numbering system provides us with the information to determine which year it should be attributed to. The first two digits are 94; therefore, this commission is dated to 1894. The last two digits are 05, meaning this was the fifth commission that year.

The catalog produced by Henry-Russel Hitchcock also assigns 1894 as the date of this house. However, William Allin Storrer, who has documented and cataloged Wright's built work, has dated the building to 1893. Thomas

Heinz and Thomas O'Gorman also date the building to 1893 in their catalogs of Wright's work. The 1893 date is derived from the date when the drawings were completed and the 1894 date from when the construction of the home was finished. There are seven plan sheets in the Frank Lloyd Wright archives for the Woolley house. Four of these sheets have a marking for a date stamp; however, only one of them is readable. Drawing number 9405.001, which is the drawing for the basement, clearly states that the date of the approved drawing was November 5, 1893, and this date is well beyond the period when Wright was working for Adler & Sullivan. Having the date stamped on the plans gives us a clue about the 9405 identification number, as the house was not finished being built until 1894. Even though this house follows the pattern of Wright's other bootleg homes, I do not think it can be counted as one. Based on the criteria that have been used to decide which homes were a part of the bootleg phase and considering that the Woolleys did not live in Oak Park until late 1893 or early 1894, this home falls outside the time frame of the bootleg phase.

The remaining commissions from the Wright archives for the year 1894 all fall well outside the period of his bootleg phase.

Chapter 3

1893: The Year of Transformation

I threw my pencil down and walked out of the Adler & Sullivan office,
never to return.
—Frank Lloyd Wright

The year 1893 started well for Adler & Sullivan; the firm was completing the final details of the Transportation Building for the World's Columbian Exposition.

There were four projects that had been started in 1892 that needed to be completed. Another three projects for which the construction documents had been completed and building permits had been received were yet to begin. The three new projects included a four-story tannery factory, which was to be built on Goose Island in Chicago. There were two projects for the Mandel brothers, who were department store owners and frequent clients of the firm. The first was a multistory addition to their retail building on Chicago's famous State Street. The second was a warehouse and stable complex that would be used to support the brothers' existing dry goods store. The store was located on what would become a significant location in the development of the city of Chicago, the intersection of State Street and Madison Avenue. The warehouse and stable were built about two lots south of that key intersection.

For Frank Lloyd Wright, the year 1893 brought on changes, as well. His second son, John Lloyd Wright, had been born on December 12, 1892. Sullivan discovered Wright's moonlighting, causing Wright's breakup with the man he looked up to as a father figure, a mentor, and a friend. This was the year that Wright became an independent architect.

Some researchers have suggested that Louis Sullivan first discovered Wright's moonlighting when he passed by a residence that was under construction that he believed had been designed by his overconfident assistant. The home that is referenced as "the one" was the Dr. Allison Harlan house, which was located at 4414 Greenwood Avenue in Chicago. This house was about two blocks northwest of Sullivan's Lake Park Avenue home.

Sullivan had come to live in the Lake Park Avenue home by an unfortunate circumstance. Louis and his younger brother, Albert, had partnered with each other to build a home for their aging mother. Albert provided the finances, and Louis provided the design. This home eventually became known as the Albert Sullivan house.

Patrick Sullivan, the boys' father, had passed away in 1884, and since then, their mother, Adrian, had been living at her sister's farm in the village of West Turin, in New York State. The brothers decided their mother should come to live in Chicago, where her two sons would take care of her. However, Adrian, who was in poor health, passed away before being able to move back to Chicago. Albert had reservations about living in the house intended for his mother, while Louis did not seem to mind at all. Louis moved into the home in 1892 and lived there through 1896.

Between his work at the firm and his work at home, Wright was quite busy in 1892 and early 1893. As has been discussed, the projects Wright worked on for the firm included the Loeb Apartments in Chicago and the Victoria Hotel in Chicago Heights. His own commissions included work in Madison, Wisconsin, and in Oak Park, River Forest, and La Grange, Illinois.

To decide which, if any, of Wright's 1893 commissions can be linked to his bootleg phase, three facts will have to be authenticated, if possible. Since it was the discovery of a bootleg house by Sullivan that caused the break between the master and the apprentice, it will be important to determine which of the three versions of the stories Wright told about his departure from the firm is "truer." It is a well-established fact that Wright left Adler & Sullivan in 1893, but when exactly did he leave the firm? The research presented will try to confirm this mystery. And finally, to link the projects Wright completed in 1893 to his bootlegging career, it will be necessary to establish the dates for these commissions, if possible.

SULLIVAN'S DISCOVERY OF WRIGHT'S BOOTLEG HOUSE

Sullivan's confrontation with Wright over his moonlighting occurred in 1893.

Louis Sullivan did not recap the events that led him to discover Wright's moonlighting work. We only have the explanations that Wright provided over the years. Unfortunately, he provided at least three versions of the events that caused the break.

The first version is found in Wright's autobiography, originally published in 1932. The second account can be found in a book Wright wrote as his homage to Louis Sullivan, after his death. This work was titled *Genius and the Mobocracy* and was published in 1942 by Duell, Stone & Pearce, New York. A third version was recorded by Edgar Tafel, who was a Taliesin apprentice from 1932 to 1941, in his book *Apprentice to Genius: Years with Frank Lloyd Wright*. In this volume, published by McGraw Hill, New York, in 1979, Tafel recounts the story, as told by Wright, of how Sullivan discovered the Harlan house.

Version One

In Wright's autobiography, he admits to designing the Blossom, McArthur and Harlan houses but not the homes in La Grange or Oak Park. He writes that "Sullivan soon became aware of them." By using the word "them," is he referring to the three homes located in Chicago?

Wright's punishment for designing these homes was Sullivan's refusal to grant Wright the deed to his now-paid-off home. Wright then asked Dankmar Adler to intercede on his behalf, but Adler's efforts were unsuccessful. Wright says the "Master" spoke to him in "none too kindly terms" and with a "haughty air." These acts were beyond Wright's ability to accept. In his autobiography, he stated, "I threw my pencil down and walked out of the Adler & Sullivan office, never to return."

In this version, it is Wright who quits, because he has not been fired by Sullivan.

Version Two

This version comes from Wright's book *Genius and the Mobocracy*, which was written over fifty years after the events took place. Here, Wright tells us that Sullivan claimed he had seen Dr. Harlan's (not the Blossom or the

THE BOOTLEG HOMES OF FRANK LLOYD WRIGHT

McArthur) house being constructed and knew Wright had designed it. On being called out by Sullivan for the work done outside of office hours, Wright was despondent. Wright believed that since he had been working overtime for the firm, he should have been able to do work on his own, as well. Wright says that he poured out his heart as he pleaded his case to the Master. He felt he would be able to repair the damage he caused if he could find the right words. He also suggests that between their first confrontation and his departure, several days may have passed.

After the initial argument between these two strong-willed men, Wright claims he "swallowed his pride," went back to see Sullivan, and tried to make amends for his transgressions, but both he and Sullivan dug in their heels and would not give the other the satisfaction of being right. Wright quotes Sullivan as having said, "Wright, your conduct has been so perfidious there is nothing I care to hear you say."

Wright carried his shame with him out the door, knowing he was the one who caused the collapse of his relationship with his dear friend. Here, again, Wright admits that he left the firm of his own volition.

Version Three

In the last version Wright created, which Edgar Tafel recorded, Wright claimed Sullivan was driving his horse and buggy from home to work one day and he went past a building site where workers were installing a foundation in a residential neighborhood. Seeing the work, Sullivan knew the design was from his draftsman's hand, and when he arrived at the office, he immediately fired Wright for his clandestine work. This version of the story is the weakest. However, Wright would have delivered this story to the rapt attention of his apprentices, more for effect than for historical accuracy.

ALL THREE OF THE stories arrive at the same conclusion: Wright left the firm in 1893.

The first version of this story is the most plausible. This version includes all three of the Chicago bootleg houses, and it was written at a time when Wright was just beginning to put the facts of his life down on paper. In the second version, Wright was trying to cement Sullivan's legacy as one of the greatest architects of the late 1800s and early 1900s. Sullivan had fallen on tough times prior to his death. Wright wanted the world to remember him for what he had accomplished during the heady days of his career and not for how he died as a penniless alcoholic in a Chicago flophouse in 1924.

WRIGHT LEAVES ADLER & SULLIVAN

To determine when Wright left Adler & Sullivan, the first thing to do is confirm what other authors have proposed.

In Grant C. Mason's book on Wright, he writes that when Sullivan found out about the bootleg houses in the spring of 1893, he confronted Wright, and after an argument, Wright walked out, never to return.

In Meryle Secrest's biography of Wright, she says that Wright went into private practice in the summer of 1893.

In the three-volume set on Wright's life by B. Koppany III, Koppany writes that the exact month cannot be determined: "Discrepancies by Wright's writing alone place his leaving the firm of Adler & Sullivan anywhere from late spring to early fall of 1893." Koppany goes on to say, "Although many authors have listed a date more precisely, at the present there is no evidence indicating a date or span of time narrower than this seven-month period."

Wright has told us in his autobiography that after leaving Adler & Sullivan, he and his confidant Cecil Corwin rented office space in the Schiller Building, but he leaves out any specific information about when they first occupied these leased offices.

On leaving Adler & Sullivan, would Wright have had the financial resources to start renting office space immediately in 1893? It seems he would not. Wright wrote in his autobiography, "From now on the young architect's studio workshop was on Chicago Avenue." Wright's home is on the southeast corner of Chicago and Forest Avenues in Oak Park. Here, Wright is telling us that he intended to be working in his own second-floor studio, not in a rented office in a downtown skyscraper.

Could Cecil Corwin have funded the move into their new offices? Wright would have been pleased to accept Cecil's financial backing for their new office space.

Of course, as always, it seems there is some contradictory information to be presented, as well. There was a short article published in the Sunday edition of the *Chicago Tribune*'s real estate section on March 14, 1894, that listed several new tenants that had begun leasing offices in the Schiller

Building. Perhaps the property management company charged with leasing space in the Schiller Building was having trouble renting offices because of the economic downturn that occurred in 1893 or for some other reason, but according to the newspaper, the building managers had decided to do just that, they lowered their rental fees, and the article said that office space was "beginning to fill up." Among the twenty-eight names listed as "new" tenants, there was a pair of individuals sharing an office, the two longtime companions Frank L. Wright and Cecil S. Corwin.

In 1892, both Wright and Corwin were listed in the Lakeside directory, with Corwin's business address as 925–218 La Salle Street, where he was partnered with George W. Maher, while Wright's address was listed at the Auditorium Building offices of Adler & Sullivan.

To create the address directories, the publishers would hire canvassers who would go door to door in the spring of any given year and record the principal names of the people working at a particular address. These canvassers took to the street in droves, so that the new directories would be ready for sale by July.

The Chicago Directory Company published both the *Lakeside Annual City Directory*, which was normally made available to the public on July 15, and the *Lakeside Business Directory*, which came out a few weeks later, on August 1.

The Lakeside directories for the year 1893 have Frank Lloyd Wright and Cecil Corwin at the same business address: 1501 103 Randolph Street, which is the address of the Schiller Building. This information puts Wright and Corwin working together in the spring of 1893. They could have signed a prorated lease in 1893 and then signed a new lease in 1894 and thus been listed as new tenants in 1894.

The Schiller Theater Building was designed by Adler & Sullivan and opened in 1891. While Wright was working on the drawings for this building, he may have envisioned himself starting his independent career on the spacious fifteenth floor of this prestigious building. For Wright and Corwin to have their offices in the Schiller Building listed in the 1893 directory, they would have had to have been in those offices before the canvassers started their work in May. Another piece of information that supports this hypothesis is that Wright was notified on May 14, 1893, that his proposal for the Madison Boathouses had been accepted. The drawings for this commission have the Schiller Building listed on them as the location of Wright's office.

This may not be empirical evidence to answer the question of when Wright left the firm of Adler & Sullivan, but these facts do begin to provide verification that Wright was in his Schiller Building office as early as May 1, 1893.

THE COMMISSIONS AND PROJECTS OF 1893

The Wright archives list seven commissions registered to 1893, including:

(1) Rocky Roost (ID number 9301), which was an island retreat built by Wright's childhood friend Robie Lamp. Wright completed a sketch of the site dated to 1893. It has been speculated that this drawing was an illustration of what was already built, rather than a construction document.

(2) Walter Gale house (ID number 9302), which has been determined to have been built in late 1893 or early 1894.

(3) The Lake Mendota Boathouse (ID number 9304), which was built in Madison, Wisconsin, during the summer of 1893.

(4) The Winslow house (ID number 9305), which Wright claimed was the first commission he completed after leaving Adler & Sullivan.

Wright had two unrealized projects in 1893, including

(5) The Lake Monona Boathouse (ID number 9308), and

(6) The Milwaukee Library project submittal (ID number 9306).

(7) Inventoried at number 9307 are the alterations to Wright's own home.

Earlier, three questions about Wright's work were put forth; below, the questions are paraphrased, and answers to each are provided based on the research that has been proposed above.

(1) Which story about his departure is "truer"? We often hear that the first answer is the best answer, and in this case, the first story Wright wrote is probably the one that is closest to the truth. Wright must have limited himself to just the facts in this version of the story. It is the most concise, and Wright was not trying to include any other points of reference; he was just retelling the story as best as he could remember.

(2) In what month did Wright leave Adler & Sullivan? Wright must have left the firm of Adler & Sullivan in March or April 1893. He may have worked in his home office for a few weeks, but to have had his address included in the 1893 Lakeside directory, he would have had to have been in this office prior to May 1. The 1894 newspaper ad that listed Wright and Corwin as new tenants was probably confirming a second full-year lease or a continuation of a partial lease from 1893.

(3) Which of Wright's completed commissions in 1893 could be from his bootleg phase? As discussed above, none of the commissions from 1893 can be included in the roster of Wright's bootleg phase.

Epilogue

I n late December 1893, Wright knew he was now an established independent architect. It would be years before the term "bootleg" and the name Frank Lloyd Wright were linked together, and the link would be made by Wright himself. Can we really confirm what he meant by that term? After Wright made his comment, another sixteen years would pass before Grant Carpenter Mason published one of the first lists of what he determined to be Frank Lloyd Wright's bootleg commissions. Often, such lists have included more commissions than were originally on Mason's list, while others have included fewer. The earliest building that may have been a bootleg commission is the MacHarg house of 1890, and the last building that is included in some lists is the Woolley house of 1894. Based on the research I have completed, I submit the following list for consideration.

Building Location	Original Client	Year	Type of Commission	Built or Unbuilt	Bootleg Ranking
Chicago	William S. MacHarg	1891	Non-Bootleg	Built	N/A
Chicago	George Blossom	1892	Bootleg	Built	First
Chicago	Dr. Allison Harlan	1892	Bootleg	Built	Fourth

Building Location	Original Client	Year	Type of Commission	Built or Unbuilt	Bootleg Ranking
Chicago	Warren McArthur	1892	Bootleg	Built	Fifth
La Grange	Henry Cooper	1890	Non-Bootleg	Unbuilt	N/A
La Grange	Robert G. Emmond	1892	Bootleg	Built	Second
La Grange	W. Irving Clark	1892	Bootleg	Built	Sixth
La Grange	Peter Goan	1894	Non-Bootleg	Built	N/A
La Grange	Orin Goan	1894	Non-Bootleg	Unbuilt	N/A
Oak Park	Thomas H. Gale	1892	Bootleg	Built	Third
Oak Park	Robert P. Parker	1892	Bootleg	Built	Seventh
Oak Park	Charles E. Roberts	1892	Non-Bootleg	Unbuilt	N/A
Oak Park	Walter H. Gale	1893	Non-Bootleg	Built	N/A
Oak Park	Francis J. Woolley	1893/94	Non-Bootleg	Built	N/A

Writing of his dismissal from Adler & Sullivan's firm in his autobiography, Wright says, "I accepted several homes on my own account, one for Dr. Harlan, one for Warren McArthur, and one for George Blossom." He does not mention any of the homes in La Grange or Oak Park. It was only the three homes located in Chicago that Wright tried to disguise his involvement in.

Could it be that it was only these three homes Wright was referring to as his bootleg commissions? The remaining homes were all commissions in which Wright had a personal relationship with the client (except for the Parker house), and these commissions were not publicized prior to their design and or construction like the Chicago commissions were. Therefore,

Wright did not need to hide the fact that they were his commissions. But these homes were designed during the period of Wright's career when he was still employed by Adler & Sullivan.

Researching when and where Frank Lloyd Wright first used the phrase "bootleg houses" has been a search fraught with dead ends, detours, and no success. The common refrain seen in other published works has been akin to the phrase "as he called them." I could not locate any first-person accounts of when Wright might have used the term "bootleg" when referring to the homes discussed here.

Mason lists ten commission that were supposed to be bootleg designs. Mason's research included his own review of Wright's drawings and personal consultations with Wright himself. Maybe it was in these interviews Wright used the phrase "bootleg houses," but Mason did not record or use this quote for his book.

The research I have conducted places the completion of the bootleg homes in the year 1892. This was the last full year Wright worked at Adler & Sullivan's firm, and it follows that this is the year he would have achieved the greatest amount of independence. During 1892, the firm of Adler & Sullivan worked on twenty different commissions, and seven of these were for projects that were located out of state. Sullivan was the face of the firm for this out-of-town business, because Dankmar Adler, a husband and father, did not like to travel, whereas Louis Sullivan, who was a bachelor for many years, was willing to work on the road.

Wright was constantly working and designing. It could be said his need to design led him to create the bootleg homes—not to secure additional income, even though this is the reason most often cited, but to feed his insatiable appetite to create art.

In 1893, Wright opened his first Chicago office in Adler & Sullivan's Schiller Building. The Schiller Building would have been a project that Wright worked on himself, and the building had a large open space on the top floor that he and Cecil Corwin converted into their offices. Wright could have had his eye on this penthouse office suite for quite a while.

Even though Wright added a full studio addition to his home in 1889, he continued to keep an office in downtown Chicago. He moved to Steinway Hall in 1896 and shared office space with fellow architects Robert Spencer, Dwight Perkins, and Myron Hunt. He then relocated his office to the Rookery Building. It was in these offices where he would meet potential clients who lived or worked in the city or who would be coming downtown on any of the train lines that served Chicago.

Wright closed his Oak Park studio in 1909, when he left for his sojourn in Europe; on his return to the States, he opened an office in Chicago again. This office was in the Orchestra Hall building. Wright's Orchestra Hall office was his last in Chicago, and he closed this office as he was leaving the United States for Japan to supervise the construction of the Imperial Hotel.

During Wright's tenure in Oak Park, he attracted clients that were successful men with young families who wanted to live in homes that were different from the homes they were raised in. They were looking for something new and distinctive. They found that the homes Wright was designing were just what they wanted. The clients for his bootleg homes were part of this upwardly mobile group, as well: families who wanted to live in prominent homes in progressive neighborhoods.

Frank Lloyd Wright had the opportunity to be tutored by three of the most prominent architects working in Chicago during the 1880s and 1890s, originally working with Joseph Lyman Silsbee and then being trained by Dankmar Adler and Louis Sullivan.

Wright learned he could complete conventional designs that would be suitable buildings for most anyone. But this was not his goal. On opening his own practice, he did not stray far from traditional themes; at first, however, he was trying innovative ideas and working toward opening the living spaces of American houses to let nature in and give families freedom from closed-off rooms and separatism. The C.A. McAfee project of 1894 shows Wright's willingness to open the home to air and light. Then, in 1895, Wright does an excellent job of interpreting the timber-framed houses found throughout Europe in the Nathan Moore house of Oak Park. In Wright's plan for the 1895 Chauncey Williams house in River Forest, he combines gable and tower roofs that are covered with wood shingles, which hark back to the styles of the bootleg period. In the year 1896, Wright completes some pedestrian designs, but he also designs the Isidore Heller house this year. This house is situated on a narrow urban lot that Wright uses to his advantage by extending his design parallel to the long lot lines. Here, Wright is beginning to move away from a simple square house to one whose design matches the environment where it is being built.

In the remaining years of the 1890s, Wright shows his ability to produce a multitude of different buildings. He also works out a design for a self-contained subdivision, where neighbors could socialize and enjoy each other's company outdoors.

In all these designs, Wright is working toward new ideas in housing, and he offers these ideas to the American public in two magazine articles in 1901. The first article is published in the April edition of the *Ladies' Home Journal* and is titled "A Home in a Prairie Town"; the second article is published in the same magazine a few months later and titled "A Small House with Lots of Room in It." In these articles, Wright expounds on the idea of living in open spaces that are linked together using wood banding and art glass windows to create a well-proportioned home. Wright's clandestine residential designs from 1892 allowed him to begin to experiment with building and design concepts without any supervision. These exercises helped him to recognize which ideas he should keep in his portfolio of designs and which he should discard.

At the start of the new century, Wright and his fellow Chicago architects left behind the old styles of architecture and developed a fresh style by and for Americans, and this style became known as the Prairie style.

Every artist must start somewhere, and Wright's early designs helped him learn proportion, flow, and construction details. And that is why these buildings are important in the story of Wright's career. They became the building blocks for what came later.

Bibliography

A. Hume. "The Story of Wool." Accessed August 29, 2020. https://www.ahume.co.uk/blog/the-story-of-wool/.

Abernathy, Ann. *The Oak Park Home and Studio of Frank Lloyd Wright.* Oak Park, IL: Frank Lloyd Wright Home and Studio Foundation, 1998.

Adkins, Jan. *Frank Lloyd Wright: A Twentieth-Century Life.* New York: Puffin Books, 2007.

Amorosino, Chris John. "Stanadyne Automotive Corporation." Encyclopedia.com. Accessed September 4, 2021. https://www.encyclopedia.com/books/politics-and-business-magazines/stanadyne-automotive-corporation.

Ancestry.com. "1880 United States Federal Census." https://www.ancestry.com/imageviewer/collections/6742/images/4240463-00480?usePUB=true&usePUBJs=true&pId=29957954.

Assignment Point. "Biography of Louis Sullivan." Accessed July 22, 2021. https://www.assignmentpoint.com/arts/biography/biography-of-louis-sullivan.html.

B., Debbie. "Permelia Holcomb Wright." Find a Grave. Accessed June 20, 2020. https://www.findagrave.com/memorial/55463980/permelia-wright.

Bayley, Guy Carleton. *An Historical Address Delivered before the Dutchess County Medical Society at Its Centennial Meeting, at Vassar Institute, January 10th, 1906* […]. Poughkeepsie, NY: Enterprise Print, 1906. https://www.google.com/books/edition/An_Historical_Address_Delivered_Before_t/GdIvAQAAMAAJ.

Beveridge, Charles E., Ethan Carr, Amanda Gagel, and Michael Shapiro, eds. *Frederick Law Olmsted: The Early Boston Years 1882–1890*. Baltimore, MD: Johns Hopkins University Press, 1977. https://www.google.com/books/edition/The_Papers_of_Frederick_Law_Olmsted/UTHSAQAAQBAJ.

Brooklyn Daily Eagle. "Fire Destroys Mansion." March 31, 1917.

Brooks, H. Allen. "Frank Lloyd Wright: Towards a Maturity of Style (1887–1893)." *AA Files* 2 (July 1982): 44–49. https://www.jstor.org/stable/pdf/29543324.pdf.

Byrd, Bonnie, and Angela Jacksack. "White Rock Collectors Association." Accessed September 4, 2021. https://theclio.com/entry/121633.

Caryle, A.S. *The Caryle Family in England and America*. New York: n.p., 1932.

Charney, Wayne Michael. "W.I. Clark House La Grange, Illinois." *Frank Lloyd Wright Newsletter* (May 1978), 4–8.

The Chicago Blue Book […] *for the Year Ending 1892*. Chicago: Chicago Directory Company, 1892. Retrieved from Hathi Trust Digital Library. https://babel.hathitrust.org/cgi/pt?id=uiuo.ark:/13960/t3610zg6k.

Chicago Daily Tribune. "Spaulding Back for Trial." November 20, 1899.

Chicago Directory Company. *Lakeside Business Directory*. Chicago: Chicago Directory Company, 1892.

———. *Plan of Re-Numbering the City of Chicago*. Chicago: Chicago Directory Company, 1909.

Chicago Landmarks. "Brewster Apartments." Accessed September 2, 2021. https://webapps1.chicago.gov/landmarksweb/web/home.htm.

Chicagology. "Chicago Burlington & Quincy Railroad." https://chicagology.com/transportation/burlington/.

———. "Kenwood Club." Accessed August 25, 2020. https://chicagology.com/goldenage/goldenage062/.

Chicago Tribune. "G.W. Blossom Long Head of Insurance Company Dies at 87." January 1, 1942. https://www.newspapers.com/clip/57284719/obituary-for-g-w-blossom-aged-87/.

———. "Obituaries." June 26, 1938. https://www.newspapers.com/clip/57805212/obituary-for-carrie-r-boardman-blossom/.

———."Raid on Globe Stock." May 3, 1897.

City of Dubuque. "History." Accessed August 25, 2021. https://www.cityofdubuque.org/1060/History.

Conkey, W.B. *Conkey's Complete Guide to the World's Columbian Exposition*. Chicago, 1893. http://livinghistoryofillinois.com/pdf_files/

Conkeys%20Complete%20Guide%20to%20the%20Worlds%20
Columbian%20Exposition.pdf.

Cook County. Cook County voter registration rolls 1892. Northeastern Illinois University, Ronald Williams Library, Chicago, IL.

Davis, James E. *Frontier Illinois*. Bloomington: Indiana University Press, 1998.

De Monchaux, Thomas. "Frank Lloyd Wright As If for the First Time." *Journal of the American Institute of Architects*, July 11, 2017. https://www. architectmagazine.com/design/frank-lloyd-wright-as-if-for-the-first-time_o.

Dietz, F. *1913: A Leaf from the Past; Dietz, Then and Now* […]. New York: R.E. Dietz, 1914. https://www.google.com/books/edition/1913/ x4YoAAAAYAAJ.

Drennan, William R. *Death in a Prairie House*. Madison, WI: Terrace Books, 2007.

Early Chicago. "G." Accessed September 4, 2021. https://earlychicago. com/encyclopedia_letter_g/.

Ehrlich, Doreen. *Frank Lloyd Wright Glass*. Blenheim Court, London PRC Publishing, 2000.

Ellickson, Dale R. "Poaching Talent." Architects Tales, December 8, 2018. https://www.architects-tales.com/2018/12/08/architects-poaching-talent-from-competition/.

Federal Census Bureau. "1870 United States Federal Census." Washington, D.C.: United States Federal Census, 1870.

Find a Grave. "Eliza Jane 'Bessie' Muirson Harlan." Accessed July 18, 2020. https://www.findagrave.com/memorial/100280427/eliza-jane-harlan.

First Unitarian Church Publication Committee. *1885–1895: Ten Years of the First Unitarian Church*. Sioux City, IA: 1895.

Frank Lloyd Wright Foundation. "Revisiting Frank Lloyd Wright's Vision for 'Broadacre City.'" Accessed August 25, 2021. https:// franklloydwright.org/revisiting-frank-lloyd-wrights-vision-broadacre-city/.

Froebel Web. "Friedrich Froebel timeline." Accessed June 22, 2022. http:// www.froebelweb.org/webline.html.

Gartner, Scott. "Frank Lloyd Wright and the Welsh Bardic Tradition." *Wright Studies* 1 (Taliesin 1911–1914): 28–43.

Geni.com. "Permelia Wright (Holcomb)." Accessed July 16, 2021. https:// www.geni.com/people/Permelia-Wright/6000000005767864486.

Gill, Brendan. *Many Masks: A Life of Frank Lloyd Wright*. New York: Putnam, 1987.

Grant, H. Roger. "Railroads." Encyclopedia of Milwaukee. March 31, 2021. https://emke.uwm.edu/entry/railroads/.

Harding, Virginia M. "Burnham, Water, and the Plan of Chicago: A Historical Explanation of Why Water Was Ignored and the Consequences of Ignoring Water." *UIC Law Review* 43, no. 2 (Winter 2010): 413–37. https://repository.law.uic.edu/lawreview/vol43/iss2/5/.

Heinz, Thomas A. *The Vision of Frank Lloyd Wright*. Edison, NJ: Chartwell Books, 2002.

Herink, Richie. *The Car Is Architecture*. Martisville, IN: Fideli, 2015.

Hidden Architecture. "Schiller Theater Building." November 4, 2019. https://hiddenarchitecture.net/schiller-theater-building/.

The History of Dubuque County, Iowa […]. Chicago: Western Historical Company, 1880. https://digitalcollections.lib.iastate.edu/islandora/object/isu%3AIowaCountyHistories_5255.

Hitchcock, Henry-Russel. *In the Nature of Materials: The Buildings of Frank Lloyd Wright 1887–1941*. Cambridge, MA: Da Capo Press, 1975.

IDFPR. "Architecture Licensing Board." Accessed July 16, 2021. https://www.idfpr.com/profs/Boards/Architect.asp.

Ingram, J.S. *The Centennial Exhibition Described and Illustrated*. Philadelphia: Hubbard Brothers, 1876. https://www.google.com/books/edition/Centennial_Exposition_Described_and_Illu/0yNDAAAAIAAJ.

Inter Ocean (Chicago, IL). "Frank Lloyd Wright." October 29, 1893. https://www.newspapers.com/image/33772075/?terms=walter%20gale&match=1.

Jacobsen, James, E. *The Architectural and Historical Resources of Dubuque, Iowa*. Washington, D.C.: United States Department of the Interior, 2003.

Johnson, Raymond. *Chicago History: The Stranger Side*. Atglen, PA: Schiffer, 2014.

Kochanov, Linda Burton. "Dr. Allison Wright Harlan." Find a Grave. Accessed July 18, 2020. https://www.findagrave.com/memorial/118287683.

———. "Mary Ester Harlan." Find a Grave. Accessed July 18, 2020. https://www.findagrave.com/memorial/121435508/mary-esther-harlan.

Kruty, Paul "Wright, Spencer, and the Casement Window." *Winterthur Portfolio* 30, no. 2–3 (Summer–Autumn 1995): 103–27. https://www.jstor.org/stable/4618497.

Lind, Carla. *Lost Wright: Frank Lloyd Wright's Vanished Masterpieces*. New York: Simon & Schuster, 1996.

Living History of Illinois and Chicago. "Hyde Park Township: A Chicago Annexed Neighborhood." Accessed March 5, 2021. http://livinghistoryofillinois.com/pdf_files/Hyde%20Park%20Township%20-%20Chicago%20Annexed%20Neighborhood.pdf.

Manson, Grand Carpenter. *Frank Lloyd to 1910: The First Golden Age*. New York: Van Nostrand Reinhold, 1958.

Marquis, Albert Nelson. *Book of Chicagoans 1911*. Chicago: A.N. Marquis, 1911.

McKean, Jill. "The Border Abbeys." Scottish Highland Trails. Accessed August 29, 2020. https://highlandtrails.com/the-border-abbeys/.

The Michigan Alumnus, vol 16. Ann Arbor: The Alumni Association of the University of Michigan, 1910. https://www.google.com/books/edition/The_Michigan_Alumnus/Pw_OAAAAMAAJ.

Miszczuk, Edward J. "John Wellborn Root." Living Places. Accessed September 4, 2021. https://www.livingplaces.com/people/john-wellborn-root.html.

Mosette, Broderick. *Triumvirate: McKim, Mead & White: Art, Architecture, Scandal, and Class in America's Gilded Age*. New York: Knopf Doubleday, 2010.

Mueller, RoseAnna, and Robert Mueller. *La Grange and La Grange Park Illinois*. Charleston, SC: Arcadia Publishing, 1999.

National Park Service. "Adler, Dankmar." Accessed June 28, 2020. https://www.nps.gov/civilwar/search-soldiers-detail.htm?soldierId=ECCAC879-DC7A-DF11-BF36-B8AC6F5D926A.

————. "Dutch Colonies." Accessed February 19, 2021. https://www.nps.gov/nr/travel/kingston/colonization.htm.

————. "Lincoln Chronology." Accessed July 3, 2020. https://www.nps.gov/liho/learn/historyculture/lincolnchronology.htm.

Nickel, Richard, S. *The Complete Architecture of Adler & Sullivan*. Chicago: Richard Nickel Committee, 2010.

Official Website of the Chicago Park District. "Galewood Park." https://www.chicagoparkdistrict.com/parks-facilities/galewood-park.

Paxton (IL) Record. February 10, 1898. https://www.newspapers.com/image/509597871/.

Permelia Records. "Praise for *The Music of William C. Wright: Solo Piano and Vocal Works 1847–1893*." Accessed August 18, 2021. http://www.permeliarecords.com/praise-for-the-music-of-william-c-wright.html.

Pfeiffer, Bruce Brooks, and Peter Goessel. *Wright 1885–1916*. Innenstadt, Cologne: Taschen, 2011.

Railway Gazette. "Election and Appointments." Accessed August 25, 2020.

Reif, Sharon. "Peter Goan." Find a Grave. September 28, 2013. https://www.findagrave.com/memorial/117768963/peter-goan.

Rose, Julie K. "A History of the Fair." World's Columbian Exposition: Idea, Experience, Aftermath. August 1, 1996. http://xroads.virginia.edu/~MA96/WCE/history.html.

Ruthmere House Museum. "The Architect." Accessed September 2, 2020. https://www.ruthmere.org/The-Architect.

Schmidt, John R. "Uptown, Past and Present." *WBEZ Chicago.* May 13, 2013. https://www.wbez.org/stories/uptown-past-and-present/beda1254-563a-474a-b4eb-f4d9f778da8c.

Scotlands People. "Church Registers." Accessed August 31, 2021. https://www.scotlandspeople.gov.uk/record-results?search_type=People&surname=BLACK&forename=JESSIE&forename_so=starts&from_year=1845&to_year=1855&surname_so=exact&church_type=Old%20Parish%20Registers&event=M&record_type[0]=opr_marriages.

Secrest, Meryle. *Frank Lloyd Wright: A Biography.* Chicago: University of Chicago Press, 1992.

Siegenthaler, Hansjörg. "What Price Style? The Fabric-Advisory Function of the Drygoods Commission Merchant, 1850–1880." *Business History Review* 41, no. 1 (Spring 1967): 36–61.

Siry, Joseph. "Frank Lloyd Wright's Unity Temple and Architecture for Liberal Religion in Chicago." *The Art Bulletin* 73, no. 2 (1991): 257–82.
———. *Unity Temple.* New York: Press Syndicate of the University of Cambridge, 1996.

Smith, Kathryn. *Wright on Exhibit: Frank Lloyd Wright's Architectural Exhibitions.* Princeton, NJ: Princeton University Press, 2017.

Sprague, Paul E. "Frank Lloyd Wright's First Architectural Design." *19th Century* 24, no. 1 (Spring 2004): 2–9.

Steiner, Douglas M. "Dr. Allison Harlan House." Wright Library. July 18, 2020. http://www.steinerag.com/flw/Artifact%20Pages/Harlan.htm#Harlan1935.

Storrer, William Allen. *The Architecture of Frank Lloyd Wright: A Complete Catalog.* Chicago: University of Chicago Press, 2002.

Taliesin Preservation. "Award-Related Wright Trivia." June 22, 2020. https://www.taliesinpreservation.org: https://www.taliesinpreservation.org/historians-corner-july-2019-pt-ii/.

Third Report of the United States Centennial Commission [...]. Washington, D.C.: Government Printing Office, 1874. https://www.

google.com/books/edition/The_National_Centennial_The_
Internationa/3rCHCu8QveQC.

Twombly, Robert C. *Frank Lloyd Wright: His Life and Architecture*. New York: John Wiley & Sons, 1979.

———. *Louis Sullivan: His Life and His Work*. New York: Viking Penguin, 1986.

U.S. Patent Office. *Official Gazette of the U.S. Patent Office*, vol. 74. Washington, D.C.: Government Printing Office, 1896. https://babel.hathitrust.org/cgi/pt?id=wu.89048454391.

University of Michigan. *General Catalogue of Officers and Students, 1837–1890*. https://books.google.com/books?id=8nIIAAAAMAAJ.

University of Wisconsin–Madison. "About the Attire." Accessed May 9, 2021. https://commencement.wisc.edu/graduate-checklist/about-the-attire/.

Wang, Lucy. "Own a Frank Lloyd Wright 'Bootleg' Gem in Illinois for $1.2M." Dwell. Accessed September 2, 2020. https://www.dwell.com/article/w-irving-clark-house-frank-lloyd-wright-f354b9d7.

Weeks, Jos. D. *Report on the Statistics of Wages in Manufacturing Industries […]*. Washington, D.C.: Government Printing Office, 1886. https://hdl.handle.net/2027/hvd.hl4p9r.

White, Sammuel G. *The Houses of McKim, Mead and White*. New York: Random House, 2007.

Wikipedia. "Infant Mortality." Accessed June 16, 2020. https://en.wikipedia.org/wiki/Infant_mortality.

———. "World's Columbian Exposition." Accessed July 16, 2020. https://en.wikipedia.org/wiki/World%27s_Columbian_Exposition.

Wisconsin Department of Public Instruction. *Biennial Report of the State Superintendent of the State of Wisconsin*. 1902. https://books.google.com/books?id=DhpNAAAAMAAJ.

Wisconsin History Day by Day. "April 15." Accessed January 12, 2021. http://www.wishistory.com/apr15.html.

Wolfe, J.M. *City Directory of Dubuque*. Dubuque, IA: 1875.

Worland, Gayle. "A New Musical Legacy for Frank Lloyd Wright's Father." *Wisconsin State Journal*, April 18, 2013. Retrieved from Capital Newspapers Inc. https://madison.com/entertainment/music/a-new-musical-legacy-for-frank-lloyd-wrights-father/article_550efbbb-3d86-5748-83a9-27675528998d.html.

Wright, Frank Lloyd. "Frank Lloyd Wright Quotes." Brainy Quotes. Accessed June 26, 2020. https://www.brainyquote.com/authors/frank-lloyd-wright-quotes.

Wright, Frank Lloyd. *Frank Lloyd Wright: An Autobiography*. Scottsdale, AZ: Frank Lloyd Wright Foundation, 1943.

Wright Society 139 (March 6, 2019). https://wrightsociety.com/issues/139.

About the Author

Bob Hartnett has had a lifelong interest in Frank Lloyd Wright's work; he found it interesting that this world-renowned architect began his career in Chicago. Hartnett has been a member of the Frank Lloyd Wright Trust as a tour guide at two of the most iconic buildings Wright created during his Oak Park years, namely the Frank Lloyd Wright Home and Studio and Unity Temple. Hartnett lives in the Chicago suburbs, where he and his wife, Lin, raised their two children.

Visit us at
www.historypress.com